Letters of
Arthur W. Pink

Letters of
Arthur W. Pink

THE BANNER OF TRUTH TRUST

THE BANNER OF TRUTH TRUST
3 Murrayfield Road, Edinburgh EH12 6EL
P.O. Box 621, Carlisle, Pennsylvania 17013, U.S.A.

© Banner of Truth Trust 1978
First published 1978
ISBN 0 85151 262 3

Printed in Great Britain by
Hazell Watson & Viney Ltd
Aylesbury, Bucks

CONTENTS

PREFACE

When Arthur Walkington Pink died in Stornoway, in the Outer Hebrides, on July 15, 1952, his passing was scarcely noticed save by a small circle of friends and the readers of his monthly magazine, *Studies in the Scriptures*. Although he had lived and preached in four countries, at the time of his death his name was practically unknown among Christians in the English-speaking world. Only with difficulty had *Studies in the Scriptures* maintained its existence through forty years, and the number of readers was seldom above one thousand.

Yet today, a quarter of a century later, the readers of his books exist in many thousands. The present publishers, for example, sold over one hundred and sixty thousand copies of three paperbacks by him in fifteen years,[1] and as a number of other publishers are also reprinting his writings (drawn almost entirely from *Studies in the Scriptures*) this first figure represents only a fraction of the total number of his writings now in circulation across the world.

It was originally hoped to include in these pages a biographical account of the author but the information to hand at the time of going to press proved too inadequate. By any standard his was a remarkable and unusual life. Born in England in 1886, converted in 1908, he spent the first twenty years of his Christian life largely in preaching, in England (1908–10), in the United States (1910–25), and in Australia (1925–28); during which period, in 1922, he also began *Studies in the Scriptures*. Apart from the help of his wife, Vera, whom he married in Kentucky in 1916, he worked single-handed on the magazine.

[1] *The Sovereignty of God*, 1961; *The Life of Elijah*, 1963; *Profiting from the Word*, 1970.

In the second decade of this century Pink appears to have begun the serious reading of authors in the reformed and Puritan tradition. By this means, next to the Scriptures themselves, he was to find himself increasingly detached from the prevailing spiritual outlook; so much so that after 1928 his opportunities to preach became very infrequent. The many changes of address, observable in these letters, between 1928 and 1936, were largely the result of his desire to be in places where he could preach as well as write. By 1936 it was finally clear to him that God meant him to give himself wholly to a written ministry. He thus settled in Hove on the south coast of England and only left there in 1940, for Stornoway, on account of the Second World War.

Along with the magazine, Pink also exercised what he believed was a God-given ministry in letter-writing. His readers became virtually his flock and from the termination of his last pastorate (in Sydney, in 1928) pastoral counsel was given to them willingly and abundantly. In one week he speaks of sending no less than 46 letters, all written in his own neat hand! While Mrs Pink typed the manuscripts for the magazine, he never had any aid with his correspondence and consequently was not able to keep copies of his letters.

For the majority of the letters in these pages we are indebted to Mr and Mrs Lowell Green of Atlanta, Georgia. For other letters we express gratitude to Mr Ray Levick of Sydney, Australia, Mr Douglas Craig of Swansea, Mr W. F. Bell, Miss Clara Brown, Mr A. V. Gilbey, Mr J. B. Culver, the Rev. W. Nicholson, and the Library of the Reformed Theological Seminary, Jackson, Mississippi.

It is probable that this book will fall into the hands of others who have letters from the author or who can supply additional biographical detail. Any material of that nature would be highly valued by the present publishers.

These letters are here printed with a minimum of editing.

The views expressed are not necessarily the views of the publisher. Arthur Pink believed that faithfulness to God required boldness and plainness of speech. If we may not always share his conclusions, his zeal for the truth is nonetheless a much needed example in the present day.

Arthur Pink was the first to confess many failings as a Christian and he wanted none to regard opinions as authoritative because they were *his*. Any personal following of his name he would have deplored. He longed to see his Saviour exalted with holy obedience rendered to His Word and if his writing could serve to bring readers, not simply in their opinions but in their lives, to be witnesses for thorough-going Christianity, there was no more that he desired.

The Publishers
March 1978

1/THE MEMORY OF THE JUST
Will Talliaferro

227 N. Creighton Street
Philadelphia
November 6, 1924

Beloved in the Lord,

It was only this noon that I received the tidings that your dear father has been called Home, for I have not the shadow of doubt that is where he now is! Busy as I am—never more so—I feel I must send you a few lines. I know you will miss him, but your loss is his gain. After so much suffering, and knowing he was prepared—'by the blood of the Lamb'—personally, I rejoiced when I learned he had left this vale of tears. Your dear father impressed me from the first time I met him. I can truthfully say that he struck me as the humblest Christian I have ever met—a blessed and beautiful adornment of sovereign grace. May you and may I be—by his enablement—'clothed with humility'.

Your father was called on to 'endure affliction' more than many, but grace kept him 'steadfast'. His homegoing will be one more attraction to draw out your heart heavenwards—may Almighty God be pleased to sanctify it to this end! It is written 'The memory of the just is blessed'—such is the memory of your father to me. May the time soon arrive when we shall meet him on high—never to part again!

The Lord willing, we expect to leave Philadelphia about January 15, spend a few weeks in meetings in California, and sail from San Francisco about March 1, for Australia—literally the 'other side of the world'! We shall much value the prayers of God's saints at this time for needed grace, wisdom, strength and guidance—we have so much to attend to before we can leave.

Remember us to all the friends, and with warm Christian love to you all, I remain,

Yours by amazing grace indeed,

2/PRAISE

Mr and Mrs Horace Coleman[1]

Millmont, Union County
Pennsylvania
April 28, 1932

Our beloved Brother and Sister in Christ,

Hearty greetings in the blessed name of him who bids us 'Giving thanks *always* for *all* things unto God and the Father, in the name of our Lord Jesus Christ' [*Eph* 5:20]. What an exalted standard is here set before us! Yet after it we should prayerfully and constantly strive. It is both for *his* glory and *our* good that we do so, for there is a wonderful power in praise to lift the heart *above* the disappointments and trials of earth. I am thoroughly persuaded that one chief reason why so many of God's dear children dwell so much in Meshech is

[1] Friends of Arthur and Vera Pink from their period of ministry in Sydney, New South Wales, Australia, where they had lived from the Spring of 1925 until the Summer of 1928. Thereafter the Pinks went to England, and then, in 1929 returned to the U.S.A. to settle in Mortens Gap, Kentucky.

because they do so little praising! A brother recently asked me what was the best way to overcome coldness of heart and a 'bound' spirit when he sought to pray. I told him to begin praising the Lord as soon as he dropped upon his knees, and if he could think of nothing else, to commence by thanking him that he was not already in Hell. I read recently of a handsome young man who returned from the war minus his right arm. His friends and relatives gathered together to commiserate him and were bewailing his loss. He turned to them and said, 'Help me to praise God that I still have my left arm'!

'Giving thanks *always* for *all* things unto God and the Father, in the name of our Lord Jesus Christ' [*Eph* 5:20]. Note the parallel between this and the language of Psalm 34:1, which shows us the unity of the two Testaments. A beautiful example of obedience to this precept is found in Daniel 6:10, 'Now when Daniel knew that the writing was signed [that he should be cast into the lions' den], he went into his house; and his windows being opened in his chamber towards Jerusalem, he kneeled upon his knees three times a day, and prayed, and gave thanks before his God, *as he did aforetime*.' How this makes manifest the *supernatural* character of Divine grace! It takes something more than an effort of will (the best the poor natural man knows of) to act thus! Compare also Acts 16:25! I think I can almost hear you whispering, 'But Brother Pink, *we* can no more bring ourselves to praise God, no more beget in ourselves the spirit of real thanksgiving, than we can make the sky pour down rain on the parched land.' That is quite true, but to dwell upon our impotency gets us nowhere, nor does it produce any fruit to God's glory. Listen: I can no more impart sound health to my body than I can create a tree. True, but (1) I *can* damage and undermine the health which I already have! (2) I *can* use those *means* which, under God's blessing, are conducive to good health. So it is spiritually. I can dwell upon my aches and pains, worries and woes, till the spirit of praise is stifled! I can read Job and Lamentations until weeping and wailing becomes a fixed habit with me. Why not turn to the last ten Psalms or the Epistle to the Ephesians? Why not 'dwell upon' God's mercies and blessings?

Sister Coleman's most welcome and helpful letter of January 24 is duly to hand. I turned it over to my dear wife to answer, but her hands are so full and I am trying to relieve her a little. Since the worldwide 'depression' began, our correspondence list has grown considerably: so many souls in trouble and perplexity, and knowing not whom to turn to for spiritual counsel and comfort. How many 'physicians of no value' there are these days; how very few really know God in an experimental and intimate way! Much wisdom is called for to deal with each different case. Some need words of rebuke, others encouragement. Some are the helpless doormats of Satan, knowing not how to 'resist him steadfast in the faith'—Revelation 12:11 tells us! Others are writhing under the chastening hand of God, and know not the remedy—Proverbs 28:13. In your case, I believe *refinement* is God's design.

We are still very busy and happy in the work of the magazine, granted much encouragement along the way, and God is faithfully supplying every need. I believe *brighter* days are ahead for the Lord's people. I look for a genuine and widespread revival, although I believe the 'present distress' must continue another year or two before there is a *real* heeding of 1 Peter 5:6. The enemy *has* come in 'like a flood', and God has *promised* that his Spirit shall 'raise up a standard against him'. 'At evening time it shall be light'! Psalm 107 holds out much hope. Above all, Jehovah is on the Throne, and his arm is *not* shortened. O that he may find us vessels 'meet for the Master's use' when his hour to lay bare his arm arrives.

Thanks very much for the various news items.

With Christian love, hearty greetings, and many prayers,

Yours by the longsuffering mercy of God,

3/EXPERIENCE THE BEST TEACHER

Lowell Green[1]

> Millmont, Union County
> Pennsylvania
> September 5, 1933

My Dear Brother in Christ,

Greetings in the blessed name of him of whom it is recorded, 'And with many such parables spake he the word unto them, as they were able to hear it' [*Mark* 4:33]; 'I have yet many things to say unto you, but ye cannot bear them now' [*John* 16:12]. These are the passages which have come to mind since prayerfully pondering yours of the 1st, to hand this morning—there being no delivery of mail yesterday. I deeply appreciate your confidence in me, and have sought grace and wisdom from above as to how to answer or advise you.

The above verses indicate that there is a growth of capacity in the Christian to receive spiritual instruction: just as the natural child cannot digest some of the things a mature person can, so it is with a spiritual child and divine things. The things which God has taught me, have, many of them, only come to me after passing through painful experiences and years of heart-exercise before God. Were I to pass them on to you, without your having gone through such experiences, you might deem them 'narrow', or strange. To illustrate: you may be accustomed to driving a car, and probably are a cautious driver; but if you met with several nasty accidents, you would

[1] The correspondence between Lowell Green of Georgia, U.S.A. and A. W. Pink began in July 1932 when Green wrote to him after reading *The Sovereignty of God*. It continued until Pink's death on July 15, 1952, although they never had the opportunity to meet.

become increasingly cautious! Experience is the best teacher! Or to come nearer home: in your letter you said, 'I have never before realized the inertia of professing Christians as I did there, facing those people'. There you had an actual experience! Suppose that same experience should be repeated a dozen times during the next six months, then you would feel differently from what you do even now. Had you read an article from my pen a year ago deploring the 'inertia' of most church-members, you might have thought I was pessimistic, or unduly sweeping and severe in my diagnosis and criticism; but after experiencing the same for yourself, you would know it was a fact.

Now in Matthew 7:14 the Lord Jesus declares there are 'few' who find the narrow way which leads to life, and were I to tell you that these 'few' are *much* fewer than nearly all the Bible-teachers, preachers, and evangelists of this day believe, you might think I was too pessimistic. Again, in Luke 12:32 Christ declares that God's 'flock' is a *little* one; and were I to tell you that it is probably *much* smaller than you now suppose, that there is a vast difference between the actual size of his flock and the totality of Christian workers and church-members, you might be far from agreeing with me. But as your experience widens and you come into closer contact with, or have business dealings with church-members, you will find that all is not gold that glitters, and that there are multitudes who call themselves Christians who have never passed from death to life spiritually—Proverbs 30:12. It is only as one comes to learn this personally, that one gradually discovers and discerns how empty and worthless is much of the zeal, toil, and activity which is going on in the religious realm; that, after all, it is but the energy of the flesh with a coat of religious paint over it.

Young people are full of life and vim, and their energies must have some outlet. Some find that 'outlet' in athletics, others in politics (electioneering etc.—for no remuneration), others in 'personal work'. Many today are taking it upon themselves to try to do what only God's equipped and Spirit-anointed servants are called to do. God's word distinctly says, 'Not a novice' [1 *Tim* 3:6], and yet in plain violation of this, thousands who have only made a profession for a few weeks or months, and have never even read through the Bible once, are urged to go out and 'do personal work' and even preach! Perhaps it may be answered, 'Well, they get results'. Only eternity will show what kind of results they are! There are thousands in the penitentiaries who once 'made a profession' under personal workers and a few years ago were numbered by those workers as among those they had led to Christ. But I rather fear I am disregarding the passages I began my letter with, and am giving you more than you can now bear or receive.

With Christian love,

Yours by God's abounding mercy

4/THE MINISTRY OF 'STUDIES IN THE SCRIPTURES'[1]

531 Thomas Street
York
Pennsylvania
December 1933

'I am the Lord, I change not: therefore ye sons of Jacob are not consumed' [*Mal* 3:6]. How grand the assurance that high above this ever-fluctuating world is One 'with whom is no variableness, neither shadow of turning' [*James* 1:17]! The great Jehovah is eternal, immutable, uninfluenced by anything out-

[1] An annual letter from Arthur and Vera Pink was always published in the December issue of their magazine, *Studies in the Scriptures*. The following is part of the annual letter for 1933.

side himself. What a satisfying object for faith to be engaged with! The immutability of God provides an all-sufficient foundation for the heart to rest upon. Nations may rise and nations may fall, empires may expand and then collapse, world conferences may convene with high hopes and then adjourn with hopes dashed; but the covenant God of the spiritual Israel *changes not*.

Because God is immutable the sons of Jacob 'are not consumed'. Who are these 'sons of Jacob'? They are those who bear the image of their spiritual father. The *spiritual* 'sons of Jacob' are they who, in felt helplessness, cling to Jehovah and cry, 'I will not let thee go except thou bless me' [*Gen* 32:26]. They are those who, experiencing many ups and downs and despite innumerable failures, are able to say, 'I have waited for Thy salvation, O Lord' [*Gen* 49:18]. Such, though harassed and frequently tripped up by Satan, are 'not consumed' by him. Such, though at times brought very low, are 'not consumed' by poverty and starvation.

Nor has this 'son of Jacob', the editor, nor the magazine, been 'consumed' by the stress and straitness of the 'hard times'. Though without any salary for the past five years, we have contracted no debts, and owe no man anything. Graciously has our faithful God continued to supply our every need, and not only so, he has enabled us to minister to more of his dear people who are in need! Nor do we believe for a moment that *our* circumstances are more favourable because we are any better than some of our suffering brethren and sisters. No indeed; in and of ourselves we are leprous beggars, entirely dependent upon the grace and mercy of our sovereign God, and every cause have we to say with the Psalmist, 'He hath not dealt with us after our sins, nor rewarded us according to our iniquities.'

Not only has the God of all grace preserved this magazine through the most difficult year the world has experienced financially during the present century, but he has also granted us many different proofs that his blessing rests upon the same. Backsliders have been restored, numbers influenced to separate from the corrupt churches, and many have been led into a closer walking with God; for all of which we ask the Christian reader to return thanks and offer praise unto him to whom alone it is due. These encouragements along the way nerve us to go on pressing forward along the path to which God has called us.

Of course, it is only to be expected that sometimes we receive letters of an entirely different character. Some of the articles which God has enabled us to write have been too searching for those who are seeking to serve two masters, and they want the magazine no more. Out of the hundreds of names which we removed from our list at the end of last year (many of whom we fondly hoped to hear from) hardly any wrote requesting that the *Studies* be sent to them again this year. We know quite well that if we would devote an article each month to 'the Signs of the Times', a page to 'Questions (on the Bible) and Answers', and would introduce one or two other such things, our little magazine would be popular in a much wider circle than we now reach. But it is our aim not to tickle the ear, but to search the conscience; not to pander to the sensation-monger, but to feed Christ's hungry sheep; not to please empty professors, but to make God's children more and more *out of love with themselves.*

But instead of being surprised that some are not able to digest 'bitter herbs' [*Ex* 12:8], we are thankful that God has enabled so many to receive them. Purgative medicine is not pleasant, either physically or spiritually, and the flesh in the Christian is no different from the flesh in the non-Christian; and only as the Spirit subdues it is any one able to appropriate that which *condemns* the flesh. In view of the fact that so much is said about the love of God, and so little about his holiness;

that so much is said about the blood and finished work of Christ, and so little about his yoke and the example which he has left us to follow; that so much is said about salvation from Hell, and so little about salvation from self-will and self-pleasing; that so much is said about the free gifts of God, and so little about the imperative necessity of an obedient walk [*Heb* 5:9]; that so much is said about the security of the saint, and so little about his working out his salvation 'with fear and trembling';—it is indeed a marvel that there is still a remnant left who *are* willing to read a magazine which honestly seeks to emphasize *both* sides with due proportion.

We are hopeful that God will be pleased to raise up other men who will, by the help of his Spirit, emphasize those portions of his truth which are now so sadly and so widely neglected. We are hopeful that God will grant a fresh outpouring of his Spirit, and are endeavouring to plead before him the promise found in the last part of Isaiah 59:19—may scores of our readers be led to *daily* plead the same! Yet, we are certain that no Heaven-sent revival will come until there is a faithful preaching *of the Law*, by which 'is the knowledge of sin' [*Rom* 3:20], and a stronger emphasis laid upon the indispensable need for *repentance*. But if God withholds a revival, then we fully expect to see fewer and fewer wanting this magazine. Would it not seem a tragedy if God continued to give the editor messages, sent in funds to print them, and had not sufficient readers to justify the publication of them? Yet this is a very real possibility! Will you not, then, pray more definitely and earnestly *for an increased circulation.*

Our list of names would be very much longer than it now is, if we would continue to send the *Studies* year after year to those who conclude they are entitled to them, merely from the fact that there is no subscription price. But though we send forth the magazine free, we are very far from getting it printed for nothing: it costs us ninety cents (three shillings and ninepence) to each person we send to for a year. Possibly there are some who conclude there is some organization or wealthy 'board' behind us. No indeed! This little messenger is published purely as 'a work of faith and labour of love', for the editor takes *nothing* out of it for his arduous and continuous services. It is supported by the voluntary gifts of the Lord's people, many of whom are very poor in this world's goods, and therefore we feel it would be a sin to use their sacrificial offerings to send the magazine to those who would trade on their generosity. Gladly do we send it to many real saints *unable* to contribute.

While seeking to press those things which make for practical godliness in the daily life, we realize there is a balance of truth to be preserved, and that there is a danger of getting the Christian too much occupied with himself and too little with Christ: therefore, if the Lord spares us and permits the *Studies* to be published through 1934, we expect to vary our note of emphasis. Having written so much of late upon the responsibility of man, a lengthy series on the high sovereignty of God should prevent our readers from becoming lopsided. This series is taken from a book now out of print, kindly loaned by a friend, *The Providence of God*, by Alex. Carson, being a most able and helpful topical treatment of the book of Esther. Then, if the Lord enables, the editor hopes to write a series on the basic doctrine of Justification, wherein we shall be largely engaged (D.V.) with the grace of God and the imputed righteousness of Christ.

Perhaps some were disappointed that we offered no comments in our columns upon 'The World's Economic Conference' which convened in London, when the representatives of no less than sixty-six nations met together to discuss the grave problems which affect their peoples. But we long that our own hearts and the hearts of our readers should be engaged with other objects. 'The world passeth away, and the lust thereof; but he that doeth the will of God abideth forever' [1 John 2:17]. What profit is there for the soul in reading over their wranglings? 'Let the potsherd strive with the potsherds of the earth' (Is 45:9). The grand consolation for the children of faith is that our God is upon the Throne, working '*all* things after the counsel of his own will'. The conference fizzled out virtually as a farce, but the Lord's purpose in it was not foiled.

On our study wall is a painted motto bearing the words, 'Thou remainest', which is of great comfort to us. During the past year quite a number of dear friends who have taken the *Studies* from the beginning have been called home; among them, several who were much used of God in the financial support of this monthly messenger. But '*Thou* remainest': he will never leave us nor forsake us, and while he has a use for this little magazine, we have no doubt whatever but that he will continue to graciously supply our every need. Hallelujah! great is God's faithfulness.

During the past year it has been the happy privilege of the editor and his devoted wife to correspond with many of our readers upon their personal problems and trials. We take this opportunity of saying that we welcome letters telling of difficulties and sorrows, and seek grace and wisdom to send a word of counsel and comfort in reply. Any time something may be obscure in our writings, do not hesitate to let us know; criticisms we always seek to weigh before the Lord. Correspondence along spiritual lines is earnestly invited. We long to redeem the time and be of help to as many dear souls as possible. We feel a real *pastoral* relation exists between us and many of our readers.

With hearty Christian greetings unto all who love the Lord Jesus Christ in sincerity,

Yours by God's abounding mercy,

5/PROFITING FROM THE WORD
Lowell Green

531 Thomas Street
York
Pennsylvania
December 18, 1933

My Dear Brother in Christ

Greetings in the holy and blessed name of him who so often declares, 'I am the Lord thy God.' May the gracious Holy Spirit enable each of us to live more and more in the realization and power of this solemn and yet glorious fact! 'If God be for us, who can be against us?' What a wonderful thing it is when we can truly say from the heart 'my *God*'!

Your very welcome letter of December 4 and 16 is to hand. I appreciate your writing me so freely. May the Lord graciously guide my pen to his glory and your good as I endeavour to reply! I am glad to hear you have been impressed with the importance of the word, and the need to obtain a direct acquaintance with and knowledge of it, for without that there can be no real growth in grace, or progress in practical godliness. In my early years I assiduously followed this threefold course: *first*, I read through the entire Bible three times a year (eight chapters in the Old Testament, and two in the New Testament daily). I steadily persevered in this for ten years, in order to familiarize myself with its contents, which can only be done by consecutive reading. *Second*, I studied a portion of the Bible each week, concentrating for ten minutes (or more) each day on the same passage, pondering the order of it, the connection between each statement, seeking a definition of the important terms in it, looking up all the marginal references, being on the look-out for its typical significance. *Third*, I meditated on one verse every day; writing it out on a slip of paper in the morning, memorizing it, consulting it at odd moments through the day; pondering separately each word in it, asking God to open to me its spiritual meaning and to write it on my heart. The verse was my food for that day, meditation standing to reading as mastication does to eating.

The more some such method as the above be followed out, the more shall we be able to say, 'Thy word is a lamp unto my feet, and a light unto my path' [*Ps* 119:105]. Let me use this verse as an example of what I mean by the third method above, of meditating on the Word. After getting the verse definitely before my mind (accurately memorizing it), I begin by asking questions: thus—Is the second clause of this verse merely a repetition of the first? That is hardly likely. What, then, is the distinct and separate concept in each clause? To help me answer, I must next ponder the exact terms found in each. In the former a 'lamp' is mentioned, in the latter 'light'; in the former 'my feet' are in view, in the latter 'my path'. While, then, the concepts of both clauses are similar, yet they are not identical.

Satisfied on this point, that the second clause is not merely a repetition of the first, I seek to ascertain the difference between them; and this, by defining the figurative expressions here used. 'Thy word is a lamp.' When is a 'lamp' needed? Not in the daytime, but at night, when it is dark. If we are more or less familiar with Scripture, other verses will now flow into the mind, linking up with the one we are pondering! For example, we shall recall how 2 Peter 1:19 tells us this world is 'a dark place'. And why is it so? because 'the Light of the world' is absent [*John* 8:12; 12:35]. Then we shall recall that 'the night is far spent' [*Rom* 13:12]—hence our need for the 'lamp'!

Second, note 'a lamp unto my feet' and not 'my eyes'—not

to *read* by, but to *walk* by. This world is not only in darkness but it is a place of great danger to the child of God, for there are gins and snares, pitfalls and precipices on every side, and unless I have the light of God's Word directing my 'feet', I am sure to fall into those snares—see Proverbs 4:19!

But I must not continue further, or I shall be sending you a small book instead of a letter! I trust I have said enough to show you what I mean by meditating on a verse of Scripture, and how to set about it.

I would earnestly counsel you to take up Psalm 119, beginning at the first verse, God willing, on January 1, and taking one verse each day; memorizing it, writing it out on a slip of paper (for your pocket), consulting it frequently through the day, pondering each word in it, praying for God to 'open' it [*Luke* 24:32], and bless it to you. As you proceed note the connection between each fresh verse you take up [in *Ps* 119] and the one or more you have previously considered. Yes, I say again, the more you follow out these methods, the more cause will you have to say, 'Thy word is a lamp unto my feet, *and* a light unto my path.' It will cast light on things around you, particularly in the religious world (where the greatest dangers abound, and where you are most likely to be deceived by fair appearances), and enable you to discern that all is not gold that glitters!

I thank you heartily for your kind enclosure. I am inscribing and mailing to you the 1933 bound volume, and one of my booklets, which I want you to read and re-read until you have mastered its contents and made them your own. I greatly appreciate your interest in the *Studies* and your desire to get others to read them. Alas, the vast majority are too busy in religious or other activities to feed their own souls! I wonder if you are acquainted with a Miss Evelyn Sorrels[1] of Atlanta:

[1] The lady mentioned by Pink eventually became Lowell Green's wife.

she receives the *Studies* and is delighted with them. I believe she is very spiritual, far above the average for the young ladies of this day.

The most accurate translation of the N.T. I know of is the Bagster Interlinear, giving the Greek in one line and a literal English translation in the next. A little Greek is useful, but it takes years of study to master it. Thankful to say all is well with us.

With Christian love,

Yours by God's abounding mercy,

6/HOSPITAL VISITATION
Wallace Nicholson[1]

531 Thomas Street
York
Pennsylvania
January 22, 1934

My Dear Brother in Christ,

Greetings in the blessed name of him whose Holy Word declares, 'A bishop ['elder'] must be . . . vigilant, sober, of good behaviour' [1 *Tim* 3:2]. Turn that into a definite prayer, also Ephesians 5:4, and as far as possible avoid those who are hilarious and given to jesting. A serious and sober demeanour is a by-product of a sober and serious mind!

Glad to receive yours of the 9th, but sorry to hear you had been indisposed: heed my instructions on how to spend Saturday afternoon and evening!

About visiting the sick, and especially indiscriminately in hospitals. In the general I would strongly advise you to greatly

[1] A student for the Christian ministry in Glasgow, Scotland.

curtail or altogether cease from it. First, you are not yet qualified spiritually—too inexperienced! Second, it is too much of a strain on your nervous system with all that you are now attempting. Third, you can spend the time to better advantage in studying or open-air exercise to keep fit! Where it is clearly a case of duty, adopt the following method of approach: 'Well, dear friend, I am both sorry and glad to see you lying upon a bed of sickness! Sorry, because you must be suffering [and endeavour to make him or her feel your sympathy]. Glad, because if God sanctifies it to you this season may be the greatest blessing you have ever had! You now have opportunity to think, to meditate, to take stock; to ponder the state and interests of your soul—God's claims—your eternal destiny.' Then ask, 'May I inquire if your mind has thus been engaged?' If they resent your inquiry, or fail to respond naturally and freely, ask, 'Would you like me to read a Psalm to you?' If, yes: read one, and then ask if they understood it. If, no; wish them well and pass on—don't cast pearls before swine! Yet, don't assume the case is hopeless: visit that person again.

Have you read the 'Dispensationalism' articles?

Thank you in his name for the kind gift enclosed.

With all good wishes,

Yours by God's abounding mercy,

7/PREMILLENNIALISM
John C. Blackburn[1]

531 Thomas Street
York
Pennsylvania
February 3, 1934

My Dear Brother,

Greetings in the holy and blessed name of him who teaches his people to pray, 'Bow down thine ear, O Lord, hear me, for I am poor and needy' [*Ps* 86:1]. Empty professors, inflated with pride, their very attitude and actions, boast that they are 'rich and increased with goods, and have need of nothing' [*Rev* 3:17]. But the real child of God, whose eyes have been opened by the Holy Spirit to see his own worthlessness, freely acknowledges that (in himself—for in Christ he possesses all things!) he is 'poor and needy', and the Lord Jesus declares, 'Blessed are the poor in spirit' [*Matt* 5:3]. May more of this poverty be our felt portion.

Yours of the 1st is to hand. I thank you heartily for your kindness in writing me at such length, and for your trouble in hunting through the second-hand book-stores on my behalf. I am very sorry I made a mistake in connection with the four volumes of Hengstenberg: unless my memory deceives me, I wrote you a postcard asking you not to loan me your copies as I had just located a set.

At the moment I know of no one enquiring for Dr Girardeau's works, but will carefully bear in mind your offer. No, I have not seen Dr Girardeau's *Discussions of Theological Questions.* I very rarely like to read a loaned book. I freely

[1] A minister in the Southern Presbyterian Church, U.S.A.

mark and index all my own. Thanks for continuing to look out for Dr Thornwell's Works.[1]

It is the 'premillennial' doctrine which I am now considerably out of love with: as a man is known by the company he keeps, so it is with a doctrine! As I studied the lives of early 'pre's' and observed those of the present day—comparing most unfavourably with the godly Puritans—my suspicions became more and more aroused, and I decided to make a fresh examination of their foundations. Knowing how easy it is to swing from one extreme to another, and how difficult it is to really approach a subject free from bias, I have sought to proceed the more slowly and cautiously. This has been going on for upwards of five years, and though I have now arrived at some positive (probably 'settled') conclusions, I have not yet definitely committed myself in print.

Approaching the subject along general lines, the first thing which struck me was the (apparent) glaring incongruity of the God-man, Christ Jesus, returning to this earth for a sojourn of 1000 years: that after being at the 'right hand of the Majesty on High' for 2000 years, he should descend to such a much lower plane! It seems altogether out of keeping with God's 'progressive' ways: i.e. from the manger to the cross, and then from the sepulchre to the highest throne that Heaven affords, and then—to go back to a mundane 'glory' seems to reverse God's 'ways'.

Assuming the above may be a prejudice created *à priori* and being willing to reject it if clear Scripture required it, the next thing which struck me most forcibly was the total absence in the four Gospels of any reference to a millennial reign of Christ on earth. Surely, dear brother, if millennarians be right, we might reasonably expect the Lord Jesus to make at least one

[1] John Lafayette Girardeau (1825–98) and James Henley Thornwell (1812–62) both served as Professors in the Columbia Theological Seminary, and gained distinction as two of the finest theologians of Southern Presbyterianism in the U.S.A.

clear reference to his coming back to earth to set up a political kingdom and reign over it for 1000 years. But where is such to be found? Take John 14:3—why did not Christ add, 'And a little later return to sit upon my throne in Jerusalem'? Why did not the two angels in Acts 1:11 add the same statement? This glaring omission struck me yet more forcibly when I noted the same held good of all the Epistles! Is it not passing strange, dear brother, that if Christ is going to be vindicated in a carnal way in the scene of his rejection, and usher in a modified form of a Mohammedan 'paradise', that not a single categorical statement to that effect is found in any of the church epistles? Why did not Paul add to 1 Thessalonians 4:16, 17—'and after the "Tribulation period" is over, he will return to the earth for his millennial reign'?

Another consideration, which I felt ought to be given due weight, was the views of the 'orthodox' (but un-converted) Jews. To a man they believe in a literal fulfilment of the O.T. promises, and look for a Messiah who shall do exactly what the 'pre's' say Christ will do in the millennium! Does not this very fact—in the light of 1 Corinthians 2:14 etc.—condemn premillennialism? Can a theory which is exactly in line with that held by unregenerate and unspiritual Jews be sound?

Next, I got down to a close examination of Scripture thereon, particularly the New Testament, though for the present leaving out of consideration the much-vexed point of a consistent interpretation of the Apocalypse. First, I noted this Christian era is the final one of earth's history: this is clearly and unequivocally established by 1 Corinthians 10:11, Hebrews 1:1, 2 and 9:26; 1 Peter 4:7; 1 John 2:18. Hence, there can be no 'millennial' age, dispensation, or era, to follow after this present one is over! Second, I noted that Christ placed the resurrection of his saints at 'the last day': John 6:39, 40, etc. Some have sought to twist that into 'the last day of this Christian age': but John 12:48 places the judgment of the wicked in this same 'last day', and thus the theory of the 'premillennialists' that a thousand years intervenes between the resurrection of the saints and the judging of the wicked is shown to be a mere dream. Their idea of two separate resurrections (separated by 1000 years) is also disproved by Acts 24:15—'A resurrection (not 'resurrections') . . . both of . . .' Third, 2 Peter 3:10 links 'the Day of the Lord' with the final and total destruction of the earth, instead of with the 'Tribulation period' as all the 'premillennialists' make out.

I may say that I have submitted the above to quite a number of premillennialists, some of them prominent ones, but none have attempted to show me I am all wrong therein. If, at your leisure, you can do so, you will be doing me a great favour.

With all good wishes,

Yours by God's abounding mercy,

8/'PROVE ALL THINGS'
Lowell Green

531 Thomas Street
York
Pennsylvania
March 15, 1934

My Dear Brother in Christ,

Greetings in him whose name is above every name. May the Holy Spirit graciously teach us to plead that name more effectually whenever we bow before the throne of grace!

Yours of the 12th is to hand. I was glad to hear from you again. In your next kindly have my last letter before you, and make some reference to its opening portion. With such a heavy correspondence, it is impossible for me to make copies of the letters I write, or to carry the substance of them in my memory for months to come. I recollect, however, that the last message I sent you was an important one, and I should be glad to know your reaction to it. It will help me if you always begin your letters by a reference to my last one.

Yes, it will be quite in order for your aunt to use chapter four in my *Redeemer's Return*. That book was written by me upwards of fifteen years ago, and were I to write on that subject today I would make some changes. More light has been given me on some things, and on others I would be less dogmatic. It is the tendency of youth to be speculative, and to accept what others say without much examination. But as one grows older, one becomes more cautious, and slower to accept man's interpretations. We all need to give more heed to 1 Thessalonians 5:21.

Yes, my Brother, indifference to spiritual things is becoming more widespread, even among those who have an intellectual interest in the more sensational aspects of the Bible. You have yet to learn that God's 'flock' is a little one [*Luke* 12:32], and that *few* are on the narrow way which leads to life. It is a painful discovery to make that not many, even of 'church members', those who attend Bible classes or Institutes, are really among the hungry sheep of Christ. There is only a 'remnant according to the election of grace' [*Rom* 11:5]! How deeply thankful we should be that God wrote our names in the Lamb's book of life before the foundation of the world.

With every good wish,

Yours by God's abounding mercy,

P.S. Thank you for answering my query about dear Sister Sorrells.

9/INCONSISTENCY AND ITS CAUSES
Lowell Green

531 Thomas Street
York
Pennsylvania
April 10, 1934

My Dear Brother in Christ,

Greetings in him whose name is above every name. May the Holy Spirit graciously teach us to plead that name more effectually before the throne of grace! It is our failure at this point which is the cause of nearly all our other failures!

Your ever-welcome letter of the 2nd is to hand. I have been hindered from replying sooner. Hearty thanks for the stamps kindly enclosed. I am glad you wrote as freely as you did, for it gives me an opportunity of understanding your case and seeking to minister to your needs more definitely.

You speak of your acting so 'inconsistently', a spiritual disease from which many of God's dear children are suffering today, and they know not the cause of the same. It is due to contrary influences being brought to bear upon them, swaying them. Those influences may all be reduced to two: those which are spiritual and those which are anti-spiritual. What so few of the Lord's people are now aware of, is the fact that the more subtle, and by far the more dangerous of the anti-spiritual forces which injuriously affect them, are to be found, not among the openly profane, nor in places which even moral worldlings condemn, but in religious circles. The reason why this is so, may be easily discovered. When a Christian is in the presence of the openly godless, he is on his guard, he prays for God to preserve him, he flees from their company as soon as he can; he asks God to cleanse him from the evil effects with which they may have contaminated him. But when he enters the religious circle, he is not so cautious because he supposes all is well there; the name of Christ is professed and the Word of God is apparently honoured, and he is unconsciously affected and infected by them. If you make a careful study of the Old Testament, you will find in the history of Israel (God's typical people) that they were corrupted far more by the Moabites and Ammonites than they were by the other surrounding nations: and the two I have mentioned were closely related to them, being the descendants of Lot, the nephew of Abraham!

What I wish to make clear is this: you may spend the early hours of the Lord's day alone with God—over his Word and in prayer. That produces a real spiritual effect upon your soul: it draws out your heart to things above, and gives you longings for a closer walk with God. Later in the day, you attend some church and mingle with those who may have 'a form of godliness', but, being strangers to God experimentally, not *walking* with him for themselves, not having spent the early hours of the morning in secret communion with him as you did, they know nothing of 'the *power*' (reality) of 'godliness'. And although they may talk of certain truths of Scripture (parrot-wise!), they are but spiritually-dead souls, and their influence upon real Christians is *anti*-spiritual, deadening, injurious.

Now it is those two totally different influences being brought to bear upon us, the one spiritual through living fellowship with God himself, the other anti-spiritual, which produce two different effects upon us, and result in two different lines of conduct from us. My Brother, it is these white-washed religious worldlings (and they may be premillennarians, fundamentalists etc.), who are so dangerous to the real

Christian! Why? Because we are influenced and affected by their ways and characteristics; their levity and lightness, their looseness and laxity. They sneer at those who seek to please God in all things, and are conscientious over little matters. For example: they make promises and break them; they fail to keep an appointment promptly, yet have no prickings of conscience over it, which tends to make *us* careless about our word. Or, they are showy and loud in their dress, which makes *us* less careful in heeding that word, 'Be not conformed to this world'. Or, they have no scruple in running into debt, which makes *us* less careful to 'Owe no man anything'. Such matters as these, and a hundred others I might mention, are regarded as trifles by the empty professors, and association with them will soon drag us down to their level and make us very inconsistent.

Inconsistencies in the Christian, then, are largely the result of the various spiritual (good or evil) influences he comes into contact with; hence the supreme importance of exercising care and caution in respect of the influences he comes under; to be suspicious of all till he proves they are really helpful; for just as physical diseases may be highly infectious, so may spiritual! And how am I to ascertain whether or not a company of professing Christians (whether in a church, a Bible Institute or anywhere else) will truly help or hinder me? In this way: does their teaching and influence make my conscience more tender or more callous? Does it emphasize the loftiness of the holy standard God has set before me and make me realize how far, far short I come of it, or does it make me pleased with myself? Does it foster pride because my head is becoming full of prophecies, dispensations, doctrines, giving me so 'much more light' than many have? Or does it foster humiliation and shame because I realize what a sad failure I am in putting into practice the things of God! That is the effect the prayerful reading of *Studies* produces; is it the effect of what you hear at the

Institute? But I really must stop. Ponder carefully what I have written and the Lord graciously bless it to you!

With loving greetings,

Yours by God's abounding mercy,

Matthew 16:24
John 8:12

10/MEEKNESS
Lowell Green

531 Thomas Street
York
Pennsylvania
Sabbath-day, June 3, 1934

My Dear Brother in Christ,

Greetings in the holy and blessed name of him who declares, 'The meek will he guide in judgment, and the meek will he teach *his* way' [Ps 25:9]. Meekness is often confused with lowliness or humility, but they are by no means identical. Humility is the opposite of pride and self-sufficiency, whereas meekness is the opposite of stubbornness and selfwill. Meekness is pliability and is the fruit of a broken heart. Meekness is the opposite of being determined to have my own way; it is an attitude of yieldedness—desiring God to work his will in and through me. Where there is true meekness (which the world, in its blindness, regards as weakness), its possessor approaches the Word with the desire to be moulded by its holy teachings, so that our characters may be formed thereby, and all our affairs, both temporal and eternal, be directed by its precepts.

Now it is the meek, and them alone, whom God promises to 'guide in judgment'. To such he imparts a stock of spiritual wisdom, which enables them to act in all things with discretion, which enables them to see through the disguises of Satan, to discern the real character of those they meet with, so that they are not deceived by outward appearances or fair words, and which makes them slow and cautious, realizing Satan is constantly placing pits and snares in their path; and thus the spiritual wisdom which is obtained from the warnings, counsels and precepts of Holy Writ, preserves them from those things which produce the ruin and destruction of those who ignore the *rule* which God has given us to walk by. The Word is an intensely practical Book. It is the chart by which we are to steer through the dangerous sea of life. Further, as my opening text affirms, it is the meek, and them alone, whom God promises to 'teach *his* way'; the way of life, of peace, of joy, leading to everlasting bliss. A theoretical knowledge of 'his way' may be obtained by reading or by hearing preachers, and that theoretical knowledge is all that millions possess. It has been self-acquired. It has not been taught them by *God*. Why do I say this, how do I know it? By the absence of spiritual *fruit*. The Lord Jesus declared, 'By their fruits ye shall know them'. It is only to the *meek* that the Holy Spirit communicates an experimental, spiritual, efficacious knowledge of 'his way'. And those who have only a self-acquired and intellectual knowledge of the truth are *not* meek; they are the very opposite. Although they may talk glibly of spiritual things; although they may be able to quote Scripture even more freely and accurately than the real children of God; yet neither their character nor their conduct is conformed to the commands and precepts of Holy Writ. How we need to beg God to make us more *meek*!

Your welcome letter is to hand. Thank you for the enclosure, which I am applying to the Magazine. It would require more time than I have available to supply the information you desire, being a long story if it were to be intelligible;

nor do I think the recounting of it would be of any real help to you. A sovereign God does not act uniformly, and he deals in very different ways with different ones. I was born in England, in 1886, and at the age of 16 entered business, in which God granted me considerable success. In 1908 he saved me in my bedroom. I knew right then that he had also called me to be his servant. I entered the ministry in 1910, and have never regretted it. In 1916 I was much in prayer that God would provide me with a spiritual and godly wife: He did. I married on November 16. You ask for a picture. I am much averse to God's servants advertising themselves, and have never allowed my photo to appear on anything which announced I was to speak. My natural picture is found in Romans 3:10–18, my spiritual picture is not yet 'developed'— see Colossians 3:3, 4. However, I am enclosing one of each of us, taken for our passports, in January 1925. I have no more recent ones.

With regard to your teaching a Sunday School class, that is a question no man is competent to answer. It all turns on whether or not you have received a call so to do from God. It is an exceedingly solemn thing for any one to stand up in the name of the Lord, handle eternal things, and undertake to teach others. Hence that word 'Be not many of you teachers, my brethren, knowing that we shall receive heavier judgment' [*James* 3:1 R.V.). There are very few places today where any child of God could teach without dishonouring and displeasing Christ! To take a class in a Sunday School identifies a teacher with that Sunday School.

With few exceptions, all the notes and comments in the Scofield Bible are unreliable and unsound. In the last 25 years I have consulted and compared many different Bibles: today I use only an ordinary Authorized (King James) Version, occasionally comparing the Revised Version and Bagster's Greek Interlinear New Testament.

The Lord be very gracious to you, keep you near himself, teach you by his Spirit, fulfil in and through you all the pleasure of his will!

With Christian love,

Yours by God's abounding mercy,

P.S. When replying, please have this letter before you and make some comment on my remarks upon Psalm 25:9: I want to see if you have really grasped them.

11/THE STATE OF THE CHURCHES
Lowell Green

531 Thomas Street
York
Pennsylvania
Sabbath-day, August 19, 1934

Beloved for Christ's sake,

Greetings in the holy and blessed name of the Lord: the One before whom the exalted seraphim bow, veil their faces in his ineffable presence, and cry 'Holy! holy! holy!' [*Is* 6]; and the One we should ever approach with lowliness and reverence. But O how little of that holy reverence do we behold in the so-called 'public worship' of the day! Why, even the heathen conduct themselves with more decency and decorum when they pay homage to their false gods. And the more we associate with the white-washed religionists of this degenerate age, the more shall we be affected and infected with their lightness and levity. One sound apple placed among rotten ones does not impart soundness to them, but causes them all to be corrupted!

Your highly-esteemed letter of the 12th now lies before me.

I praise God that he condescended to speak to your heart through what he enabled me to write on June 23rd. I kept no copy. But spiritual meekness is a grace which is of 'great price' in the sight of God [1 *Pet* 3:4]: it is part of the 'fruit of the Spirit' [*Gal* 5:22, 23]. We are bidden to 'seek meekness' [*Zeph* 2:3]. If you consult a concordance, you will find that many precious promises are addressed to the *meek*. Meekness is learned from Christ—Matthew 11:29!

You ask me to write you very definitely 'about living a life of victory over known sin'. You may have observed that I say comparatively little thereon in my writings. First, let me say frankly that I have little patience with most of what has been taught during the past twenty years about 'The Victorious Life'! Those who have most prominently advocated and propagated it are discredited in the eyes of competent judges, for they are radically unsound on fundamental doctrine! They are Arminians to a man; they deny the absolute sovereignty of God, his eternal choice of an elect people, and that Christ bore their sins only. They deny the total depravity of man, for they insist that he possesses a free will and can accept Christ and be saved by a decision of his own; thus directly repudiating *God's* Word, as found in John 1:13; 6:44; 8:36; Romans 9:16, and other passages. And where any preacher or teacher is unsound on these basic truths, *no* confidence must be placed in him on any other subject. If he is all wrong at the foundations, his superstructure is bound to be faulty.

Alas, also, real servants of God, sound teachers, have now almost disappeared from the earth. 2 Timothy 4:3 is now fulfilled before our eyes; men 'will not endure sound doctrine'. They will still tolerate what is called evangelism, they will listen eagerly to a talk on 'the signs of the times' (made up of sensational items culled from newspapers with a little Scripture ingeniously fitted in to give respectability), they will listen to missionary addresses: but *sound doctrine* they will not endure!

Hence we have, in that divine declaration, an infallible test by which the poor child of God may *measure* things in the Babel of tongues now going on in Christendom! That *test* is this: anything which *is* endured today in the religious world cannot be sound doctrine; anything which is approved of, well attended, popular, is *not* 'sound doctrine'.

Where *God* works, he always does so consistently with his own Word. What I mean by that is this: when *he* raises up, equips, and sends forth one of *his* servants, that servant will necessarily preach the *Word*, and denounce all that is opposed to the Word: hence, his message is bound to be *un*popular, in fact, hated by all who are not regenerated. Was it not thus with the Old Testament prophets? Would even the Israelites of their day endure *sound* doctrine? Would they do so when the Lord Jesus preached it? Would they when the apostles taught it? Would they in the time of Luther and Calvin? And poor, fallen human nature is the same now! Mark it well, my dear friend, that the people to whom the Old Testament prophets, Christ, and the apostles preached were not irreligious! No, indeed, far from it! They were very religious: but they were determined to have a religion of their own, which suited them, and they would not tolerate anything which condemned them. So it is now.

Even 'orthodox' Christendom now has a religion of its own. True, there is quite a little in it which is scriptural—as there was in the case of the Pharisees, as there is in the case of the Romanists—but there is also much that is unscriptural and *anti*-scriptural, and it is that which proves (to one governed by the Word) that the Holy Spirit is not behind it. The Holy Spirit has commanded, 'Let your women keep silence in the churches' [1 *Cor* 14:34]; then will the Holy Spirit now prompt testimony meetings and mixed prayer meetings where women are encouraged to speak before men? It would be blasphemy to say so. And yet there are places and groups today who seem to be very much devoted to the Lord, very spiritual, very sound, very much concerned about the salvation of sinners and a 'separated life' for Christians, and these people have their testimony and fellowship meetings, and surely they are not wrong! *Test* them! God *commands* us to 'try' or 'test' them. See 1 John 4:1, and observe how Christ commended the church at Ephesus for testing ('trying') those who claimed to be apostles—Revelation 2:2.

But *how* are we to test them? Apply the principle of 2 Timothy 4:3; to see if they are teaching 'sound doctrine'. One part of that 'sound doctrine' is the *silence* of women in the churches—compare 1 Timothy 2:12 and 13—read to them 1 Corinthians 14:34 and see if they will endure that! If their hearts are in subjection to God, they *will*: they will thank you for enlightening them, they will confess and forsake their error. But if their hearts are *not* in subjection, if in spite of all their seeming sanctity and devotion to the Lord, they are really determined to have their own way, they will quibble, argue, and refuse the light you bring them from God's Word. Try it out, and see for yourself! Approach them meekly and lovingly: tell them that 1 Corinthians 14:34 is so plain it cannot be misunderstood, that it is one of the divine commands for us to *obey*. Take your stand on that verse firmly and you will not only find that its 'sound doctrine' will not be 'endured' by them, but they will quickly show that you are not wanted by them!

As more light is granted you from the Word, as you are more regulated by its precepts and commandments, as you form the habit of *testing* people and religious movements by the Word—by which I do not mean sitting in judgment upon them, but measuring them by its sound doctrine—you will more and more discover the truth of that word, 'he that increaseth knowledge increaseth sorrow' [*Eccles* 1:18], which is something else the flesh does not welcome!—sorrow' over the tragic state that poor Christendom has fallen into, and that will bring you into the 'fellowship of his sufferings' [*Phil* 3:10], for *he* wept, not over Egypt, or Greece, but over Jerusalem!

Yes, it will bring you among the despised but favoured company of Ezekiel 9:4! And then, and not till then, will you be likely to *cry* unto God, 'O Lord, revive thy work in the midst of the years, in the midst of the years make known; in wrath remember *mercy*' [*Hab* 3:2]. And while others are running around from one meeting to another, having their good time by 'fellowship' with congenial young people; and while others are lusting after the fleshpots of Egypt, making a god of their belly, and indulging the lusts of the flesh in listening to the radio, laughing and joking with backslidden saints, you will be on your face before God in secret, *pleading* his promise in Isaiah 59:19!

O that it may please the God of all grace to fit you to become a secret but effectual intercessor, one whose groans and tears have power with God! Such have been my fond hopes, concerning others, only to have them bitterly disappointed because they were *unwilling* to mortify the flesh and pay the price. My greatest grief today is that, after moving so much from place to place, travelling entirely around the world, I do not know of a single Christian (apart from my dear wife) who gives the slightest real promise of becoming a prevailing intercessor before God. Numbers I had hoped might become so, but my hopes have been dashed to the ground, until at times I feel like burying myself in some isolated retreat, where I would never meet another Christian on earth again. They are all like those referred to in Ezekiel 33:31-33: 'They come unto thee as the people cometh, and they sit before thee as my people, and they hear thy words, but they will not *do* them: for with their mouth they show thee much love, but their heart goeth after their covetousness. And, lo, thou art unto them as a very lovely song of one that hath a pleasant voice, and can play well on an instrument: for they hear thy words, but they *do them not*'!

Yes, they will sit at one's feet and admire even searching and solemn teaching, admire the courage and faithfulness of him who gives it out, and say 'what a privilege' to sit under such a ministry. They will heed some of the teaching and make a general application of it to themselves, but when it comes to detail, and putting right particular failings and sins in their own lives, when the shoe pinches their own foot, they *refuse* to act. They criticize God's servant behind his back, and undermine his influence with others. They still cling first to their own favourite idols. And yet some of these very persons suppose they can have power with God in intercession. Poor deceived and deluded souls! They think they can spend one hour listening to the radio, or engaging in light jocular conversation with others, and then retire to their rooms and pray! It is not words which God pays attention to, but heart-groans and tears! And no heart can pass from worldly amusements and frothy talking unto spiritual *mourning* before the thrice holy God. He requires *reality*, and only his Spirit working in one whom *he* is not grieved with, can produce that reality.

O, my dear brother, my own soul is weighed down, almost overwhelmed, as I behold the *lack* of reality in almost all of those to whom I have sought to minister. This is the chief reason why I am leaving the States. God's blessing has been and now is upon my written ministry in a most unmistakable and gracious way; but my personal ministry through direct contact is almost a complete failure. But, as the closing verse of Ezekiel 33 solemnly declares, 'And when this cometh to pass, (lo, it will come) then shall they know that a prophet hath been among them.' And there I must leave it; in the hands of him whom I have earnestly sought—amid much personal weakness and failure—to faithfully serve.

I rather fear that this letter will be somewhat disappointing to you. But as I sat alone in my room this morning, reviewing the past few years, and then realizing how soon I shall have left the States for ever, I hardly felt in the mood for writing a formal letter. As you had so opened your heart to me, I felt like uncovering mine a little to you. None but God knows the sorrow and anguish that my dear wife and I have experienced over some of our best, kindest and dearest friends; those who have freely, unselfishly, frequently ministered to us in many ways temporally, and to whom we so longed to be made a real and rich blessing spiritually, not in a merely ordinary and general way, but to see them actually enter into God's *best* for them. Perhaps our prayers for them may be answered and our longings for them realized, after we are far removed from them all. Forgive me, then, if I have written too freely. At any rate it will afford you some insight into the inner experiences of a servant of God.

The Lord willing, I hope to write you again before the month is out, replying more definitely to several things in your letter. Meanwhile, I enclose one of my booklets on Romans 7.

With Christian love and every good wish, I remain,

By God's abounding mercy,

12/TRUE AND FALSE RELIGION
Lowell Green

559 Dupont Avenue
York
Pennsylvania
Sabbath-day, September 2, 1934

My Dear Friend,

Greetings in the holy and blessed name of him who bids us 'grow in grace' [2 *Pet* 3:18]. O how very few have any true conception of what spiritual growth really is! Multitudes of professing Christians in this cloudy and dark day repeat sentences of Holy Writ and no more understand their import than do the telegraph wires the words they transmit! Years ago, I was helped by a sentence I read, quoted from a quaint and altogether illiterate old woman, but who was evidently taught of God. She said: 'When a Christian grows in grace, his growth is the same as the growth of a cow's tail. The more her tail grows, the nearer the ground it comes'! And my beloved Brother in Christ, that is true spiritually; the more we really grow in grace the more we take our proper place—in the dust before God! The more we grow spiritually, the more out of love with ourselves we become! The more we grow spiritually, the less will we boast of what 'I have done', and the more will we speak (when in the presence of those who can understand and appreciate—and, believe me, they are few and far between) of what great things *the Lord* has done for us— his mercy is stooping to pick up so vile a wretch; his long-suffering in bearing with one so incorrigible.

I had a sweet illustration of this come to my notice a few days ago concerning a person I had not seen for two years, one whom I have sought by God's grace to help by correspondence. In the course of a conversation, he said: 'Brother Pink, I don't want to appear a hypocrite before you! From my letters, you may think I'm a spiritual and lovely character; you don't know me: I've a beastly disposition'. O, those words made me praise God fervently. They furnished clear proof of that dear fellow's spiritual growth! Alas, had many of these self-righteous Pharisees and 'Victorious life' people heard him, they had looked on him with something approaching to scorn. I mention this to let you see that all the *real* children of God speak the same language. *Sheep* don't bark and make a loud noise, but they all bleat! Have you ever pondered Matthew 11:29? How completely out of accord with even the orthodox and fundamentalist actions of Christendom today! 'Learn of *me*' says Christ. And what is it he would have us 'learn' of himself? How to be a 'successful soul-winner'? How to do great things? How to become popular in Christian circles? *No* indeed; the very opposite—'for I am *meek* and *lowly*'. O, my dear Brother, these are things we have to *learn*, for by nature we are utter strangers to them! Nor is there the least likelihood of our acquiring them through contact with the frothy professors of the day. *No*, they can be learned only from *Christ*. And notice too, and notice it thoroughly, that before we can learn these things, these spiritual graces, from Christ, we have first to *take* his *yoke* upon us; the yoke being a figure of subjection—fully surrendered to his lordship, *his* will ruling and guiding us.

My earnest advice is for you to have little or nothing to do with the people of the religious world today. They cannot help you spiritually, and where they help not, are bound to hinder! But be much in prayer and on your guard against a holier-than-thou attitude. If we are not very watchful, separation soon leads to self-righteousness. On the other hand, association with empty professors soon corrupts and paralyzes true spirituality. Prayer, reading and meditation will do far more for your soul—with God's blessing on the same—than attending meetings and being active in 'Christian service'.

God willing, we sail on the 5th at 5 p.m., due Southampton on the morning of the 11th, and reach our destination that afternoon or evening. Kindly pray that God will so undertake for us through the Customs at Southampton, that we will not be held up there and so miss our train for Cheltenham; that he will lead us very definitely to the peaceable habitation of his providing; and that it may please him to open for us in England doors of utterance. Our journey there is by faith, for there is nothing in view to sight. God has freely provided us with funds.

The Lord has markedly and wonderfully answered prayer on our behalf during the past few weeks. Never before has the disposing of our furniture, packing up my large library (weighing over half a ton!), and making all necessary arrangements, gone so easily and smoothly. I am thankful to say both of us feel quite fit.

The Lord continue to be very gracious to you; guard, guide and gird you!

With our united love and every good wish,

Yours by God's abounding mercy,

Psalm 37:4

13/THOUGHTS IN MID-ATLANTIC
Lowell Green

On board R.M.S. *Majestic*
Sabbath-day, September 9, 1934

My Dear Brother in Christ,

Greetings in the holy and blessed name of him who 'hath done all things well' [*Mark* 7:37]. It is a sure proof of divine grace ruling within us when we are able to say this from our very hearts, even when to sight and sense things seem (to us) wrong and ill. Divine wisdom makes no mistakes, and divine power cannot be thwarted by either man or Devil. And when faith is in exercise, occupied with God's perfections, then our language must be, 'He hath done all things well'.

We had a pleasant railroad journey to New York, and on arriving at the dock were happy to find that our six boxes (of books) and three trunks (sent by freight) had all arrived safe and sound. Our ship left promptly—5 p.m. Wednesday—and we remained on deck while we sailed down the river and passed the Statue of Liberty. It was with mingled feelings I watched the fading shore, for although born and educated in England, I have spent less than two and a half years there since 1910. My parents have been called home, and almost all my Christian friends are in the U.S.A.

The sky was almost cloudless and the sea quite calm throughout Thursday and Friday. Yesterday it was overcast and raining, though the sea remained calm. Today the ocean has been rather rough, and I expect will remain so for the remainder of the voyage, two-thirds of which now lies behind us. Today

I have remained in our cabin, but have not been sick—head a little giddy, that's all.

As far as we can see, there are no other children of God aboard. Our fellow-passengers are given up to sport, bathing, dancing, etc. We have kept quite to ourselves. This morning they held 'Divine Service', conducted by the captain. Many would be shocked to hear we did not attend and join in thanking the Creator for journeying mercies. But I think you will now understand. We simply could not have fellowship with those who last night drank and danced, and this morning went through a 'form of godliness'. But we did endeavour to worship our gracious Father in the privacy of our own cabin! I have mentioned this to you (and in none other of my letters) to press on you the force of Ephesians 5:11, 2 Timothy 3:5. It is in just such matters that Christians either miss or enter into God's best for them. May he graciously deliver you from the fear of man and keep you in that narrow way which alone leads to *life*!

At first you may feel a great distance now separates us, but after we have exchanged a few letters (D.V.), it will not seem so great. At any rate, we can still meet in spirit at the mercy-seat.

The Lord bless and keep you very near himself.

With Christian love,

Yours by God's abounding mercy,

14/THE SABBATH AND GUIDANCE
Lowell Green

> 31 North Place
> Cheltenham
> England
> Sabbath-day, October 14, 1934

My Dear Brother in Christ,

Greetings in the holy and blessed name of him who has commanded us, 'Remember the sabbath day, to keep it holy. Six days shalt thou labour and do all thy work: but the seventh day is the sabbath of the Lord thy God: in it thou shalt not do any work' [*Exod* 20:8–10]. This is one of the Ten Commandments which the Lord God himself wrote upon tables of stone —signifying their permanent nature and abiding authority. If it is still wrong for us to break the other nine commandments, it must still be wrong to break this one on the Sabbath. It is significant to note that this is the only one of the Ten which opens with the word 'Remember', as though men had the greatest tendency to forget it! That word 'Remember' also plainly intimates that this Sabbath commandment was not given at Sinai for the first time, for the Israelites of Moses' time could not 'remember' something which they had never heard of before! I mention this because erroneous teachers are fond of declaring today that the 'sabbath' is entirely Jewish, that it began and ended with the Mosaic dispensation. This is a serious mistake. The command to keep the sabbath holy did not begin at Sinai, as its opening 'Remember' clearly tells us. The word 'remember' takes us back to Genesis 2:2–3, where we find that immediately after the creation of man, the Lord God did three things: (1) He 'rested on the seventh day'—why? because he was weary? Of course not, but as an example to all his creatures. (2) That the Lord God 'blessed the seventh day'—why?—to teach us that divine approbation rests upon those who emulate the example which the Creator himself has set. (3) That the Lord God sanctified it: which means that he set it apart for a sacred use, for that is what the word 'sanctified' means in Scripture. Thus from Genesis 2:2-3 we learn that the Lord God instituted the holy Sabbath two thousand years before Israel reached Sinai. Another proof that some modern Bible-teachers err radically and seriously upon this subject, is found in the plain words of our Lord Jesus: 'The sabbath was made for *man*' [*Mark* 2:27], and not for the Jew alone.

Coming back to Exodus 20:8–11, notice carefully that it says: 'Six days shalt thou labour and do all thy work, but the seventh day is the sabbath'. But it does *not* say 'the seventh day of the week'—that is the error of the Seventh Day Adventists. Six days of work—without specifying which days—and then a seventh of rest. The Jews worked from Sunday till Friday; we from Monday to Saturday.

Now as you have learned in connection with other subjects, no one passage stands alone, but Scripture interprets Scripture. So it is with the words 'in it [the Sabbath] thou shalt not do any work'. In the light of Christ's own teaching and example in the four Gospels, we learn that works of genuine necessity and works of mercy *are* permissible, but *no* others. A reference to other scriptures, such as Isaiah 56 and 58 shows our own (natural) 'pleasure' is to be set aside on the holy Sabbath, and our whole thought and time are to be given to the things of the Lord. History most emphatically records that those nations which have most strictly kept the Sabbath have been prospered, spiritually and temporally, by God. The same is true of a family or of an individual. I attribute very largely the temporal blessings we have had in the past 18 years to our strict observance of the Sabbath, for during all that time my wife has never cooked a hot meal on that day—the woman as well as the man needs one day of complete rest out of each seven! She prepares the food on Saturday, and we eat it cold—except a drink of hot tea—on Sunday. Sunday newspapers and all secular concerns should be rigidly banned on the Sabbath. I have a booklet on the subject if you would like one, although it deals with it more doctrinally (argumentatively), than from the practical side. If all is not clear to you now, let me know.

> *A Sabbath well spent*
> *brings a week of content,*
> *and strength for the toils of the morrow.*
> *But a Sabbath profaned,*
> *whate'er may be gained,*
> *is a certain forerunner of sorrow.*

Your good letter of September 23 is to hand. We are indeed grateful to you for your prayers, and my last letter will show how God has answered them. We are very comfortable in our new abode. We had a young preacher for five days, from Scotland—one whom I had not met before, but with whom I have corresponded (as with you) for the past four years. We had a blessed time together!

I was happy to hear that both you and your father had withdrawn from the 'churches', and my earnest counsel now is to go mighty slowly [Is 28:16], before you even think of joining another. Investigate thoroughly, and find out what is going on behind the scenes before you apply. A sound man in the pulpit is no proof the membership is a regenerate and spiritual one!

About salesmanship! Commit the matter definitely to the Lord and leave it with him. If the position is offered to you unsought, take it as from God. From the human side of things, a year or so on the road would be good experience, giving you a closer acquaintance and wider knowledge of human nature. But make it plain to the Sales Manager that you cannot mis-report any article in order to obtain business. There is an awful lot of that being done today. If you trust-fully commit the whole matter to the Lord, asking him to block the opening for salesmanship if it is not for his glory and your highest good, and the way opens, you may safely take it as God's answer to your prayers. I must close now as I expect Christian friends here for the evening. The Lord guard and guide you!

With Christian love from us both,

Yours by God's abounding mercy,

15/ON BOOKS AND BAPTISM
Wallace Nicholson

31 North Place
Cheltenham
Sabbath—October 14, 1934

Our Dear Brother in the Lord,

Greetings in the blessed name of Christ: may the Holy Spirit graciously make him more real and precious to each of our needy hearts, and grant us the sorely-needed grace to love him more fervently, commune with him more constantly, and obey him more unreservedly. He is 'worthy' of our *best*!

Your welcome letter of the 9th is to hand. What sort of a journey did you have to Glasgow? Did you see anything of Mr McKendrick? I think he returned to Scotland the same morning. We were very glad to hear you had passed in Moral Philosophy—praise God: he has been very good to you. For the immediate present I feel we should quietly and trustfully look to the Lord for the meaning and fulfilment of his purpose in bringing us to Cheltenham. Two new ones were out last Wednesday p.m. (we had 14 in all), and the Lord granted great liberty: we were encouraged.

I have finished reading through the volume you kindly brought me by Thornwell and later, D.V. would like to see the companion volumes. There are some excellent things therein, yet some I do not like. He is faulty, to say the least, in his discussion of Repentance—pages 37–39. I will not enter into detail about his analysis of supra- and sub-lapsarianism: his last sentence of first paragraph on page 24 exhibits the weakness of his system—a purpose to *glorify himself* rather than 'a purpose to *save*' was the *starting point* of God's decrees! The supra-lapsarian system makes God the beginning, centre and end thereof; whereas sub-lapsarianism makes Man the centre and circumference. He is fine on 'The Priesthood of Christ', and 'The Nature of Salvation'. I observe that he teaches plainly the *direct* action of the Holy Spirit on the soul—therein concurring with my articles on 'The Spirit Quickening'!—see pages 309 and 310. On the whole I am rather disappointed with his style—he is too philosophical and not sufficiently expository to suit my taste.

I believe you would be well advised to substitute for the 52 volumes by Calvin, the 22 by Manton, 16 by Owen and 12 by Goodwin, for I am sure that if you are spared to give the same *a careful reading* right through, you would get more than twice as much out of these three as out of Calvin. There is little else among those books I would counsel you to procure.

I have read the book you kindly sent me by Edwards,[1] and am returning the same with thanks. During the last 25 years I have read prayerfully and carefully *many* works, constructive

[1] *Candid reasons for renouncing the principles of Anti-Paedobaptism*, Peter Edwards, 1888.

and controversial, on the vexed question of Baptism, so that I am thoroughly cognizant of the arguments on both sides. I do not feel it is the Lord's time for me to discuss this subject with you, as I do not wish to bias or unsettle you in any way thereon. I do not regard it as in anywise a vital matter, and it ought never to disrupt or even disturb *Christian* fellowship; yet, personally, I dare not quench the light which I believe God has given me thereon. I can only add that, my reading of Edwards has not shaken my convictions to the slightest degree.

Will your studies in the University this year be limited to two subjects? If so, you should not be so crowded, and have more time for sermon preparation. Write us from time to time as you are able.

With every good wish and Christian love from us both,

Yours by God's abounding mercy,

16/READING, CURRENT TRENDS AND MARRIAGE
Lowell Green

31 North Place
Cheltenham
England
Sabbath–day, December 2, 1934

My Dear Brother in Christ,

Greetings in the blessed name of the Lord! May the Holy Spirit graciously constrain us, more and more to 'acknowledge him' in all our ways! I feel led to begin with the same verse which opens your good letter of November 11. I note that later on you mention that you hope to complete your second reading of *The Sovereignty of God* before this year expires, and that you are assured there is 'no other resting place for the heart'. It is much to be thankful for when the understanding is enlightened to perceive the fact of the absolute supremacy of God, that he is indeed 'the Most High', Governor of heaven and earth, Imperial Disposer of all creatures and all events. What effect should the intellectual apprehension of this fact produce in us? What ought to be the practical outcome of it upon our daily lives? This: 'In all thy ways acknowledge him'. First, I 'acknowledge him' as my Sovereign Lord, as the One who has the unquestioned right to entire submission from me. Second, I 'acknowledge him' as the One upon whom I am completely dependent for all things, without whose blessing nothing I do can possibly prosper. Third, I 'acknowledge him' as the One whom I desire to honour and glorify, seeking to please him in every detail of my life.

It cannot be expected that those who repudiate his sovereign supremacy should take this attitude before him. No, they are free-will agents, deciders of their own destiny, and therefore lords over themselves. Hence *self* governs all their thinking, planning, and actions. But it should be far otherwise with those who, by distinguishing mercy, have had their eyes opened to see God upon his *throne*. Their daily prayer must be for God to graciously bring their hearts under the power of this great truth, that they may conduct themselves *as* the submissive and loyal subjects of this Sovereign, and that by 'acknowledging him in all their ways'. May it be so with each of us for his name's sake!

It is most important at your present stage of life that you 'give attendance to reading' [1 *Tim* 4:13]. As soon as you complete *The Sovereignty of God*, I want you to take up, carefully and systematically, my twenty-four articles on 'The Satisfaction [Atonement] of Christ' in the 1930 and 1931 *Studies*. Form the habit of definitely seeking God's help and blessing each time you are going to read, asking him to prepare your heart, to make it receptive and retentive. After

the reading, spend a few minutes in meditation, seeking to fix
in your mind the leading truths which have engaged your
attention, asking yourself how you may improve them in a
practical way—i.e. how to turn them to profit in your daily
life. I was glad to hear of your procuring Calvin's *Institutes*;
much in that book is most helpful! The mastering of a few
such works would mean far more to you than a hurried and
superficial reading of hundreds of other books! In that way
you would be fortified against the errors propagated today by
leading Bible-teachers, who have just sufficient truth to deceive
the ignorant, those who have not taken sufficient time to
become established in the faith; and that cannot be accomplished in a few weeks!

Quite recently I received a letter from a dear Sister in
Toronto, who, sick at heart, has felt reluctantly compelled to
withdraw from the religious world—apostate Christendom.
In it she states, 'I myself heard Dean Gray (head of the Moody
Bible Institute, Chicago) say from a public platform, "No
matter what you may do, from stealing to murder, you will
be saved for ever".' And the awful thing is, my dear Brother,
that thousands of 'Fundamentalists' applaud such Satanic error,
blindly imagining that such teaching magnifies the grace of
God in the eternal security of his saints. But God does *not*
preserve his people in the ways of sin: he preserves by working
in them a hatred of such sins! I am well aware that it sounds
a most terrible thing to say, but it is now my settled conviction
that men like Pettingell, Gray, Gaebelein and others are doing
just as much harm as Fosdick and the higher critics! Nor have
I much patience with those (like the editor of the magazine
you mention), who would get the Lord's people occupied
with such matters as a 'Partial Rapture', or 'The Church going
through the Tribulation' (a number in England are now
agitating this question). It makes me think of Nero fiddling
while Rome was burning.

Many thanks for the strip of photos. I trust the study of them will enable me to minister more helpfully to your needs; thank you also for your continued prayers on our behalf. Having spent almost the whole of my Christian life in the States and in Australia, I am virtually an unknown man here, and unless the Lord is pleased to move someone of prominence to use his influence on my behalf, it is likely to be a very slow matter to obtain a hearing. However, all things are in *his* hands. What a mercy! Nevertheless, I shall appreciate prayer that it may please him to show himself strong on our behalf and open doors of utterance for me. You will rejoice to know that on November 30 (our usual date) we closed the Magazine year for 1934 with the best credit balance we have ever had—Hallelujah! And I believe by December 31 we shall have the twenty per cent increase of circulation for which we have prayed daily for ten months past. If spared, I hope for a still further increase in 1935.

The question of choosing a wife is not easily answered. It is a very serious and solemn undertaking, and calls for much waiting on the Lord, for discernment of his best for us. Personally, I acted very slowly, being thirty years of age before I entertained any serious thoughts on the matter. But God does not deal with all alike! 'A prudent wife is from the Lord' [*Prov* 19:14] is what guided me, and I begged him to direct me to such, and he did. No man ought seriously to contemplate matrimony until (1) He is in a financial position properly to support a wife—otherwise he is 'tempting' the Lord and presuming on his providence. (2) Till he has, in some goodly measure, learned by grace to rule his own spirit [*Prov* 25:28], otherwise he will be a plague to his partner and not a 'helpmeet'! (3) Until he is sure that God has brought him into contact with a truly regenerate girl, who is likely to be congenial, equally yoked, and a help to him. In seeking a wife neither good looks nor money should influence him. Moral qualities and spiritual graces last when physical beauty has faded and money taken to itself wings. There are real advantages and some disadvantages in the wedded state. The character of the times in which we are living calls for double caution. It is a very solemn thing to bring children into the world these days! Please feel quite free to renew this question —in detail— if you wish.

The Lord graciously keep you near himself and then you cannot go wrong. Read carefully my current articles on 'Divine Guidance'.

With much love,

Yours by God's abounding mercy,

Psalm 27:14

17/PROBLEMS IN CHRISTIAN SERVICE
Lowell Green

31 North Place
Cheltenham
England
January 23, 1935

My Dear Brother in Christ,

Greetings in the blessed name of him who assures us, 'Delight thyself also in the Lord, and he shall give thee the desires of thine heart' [Ps 37:4]. There is an important and intimate relation or connection between the two halves of this verse. The more we truly 'delight ourselves in the Lord' and earnestly seek a close communion with him and a fuller conformity to his will, the more will the 'desires of our hearts' be prompted and moulded by him, and consequently, the more will we ask only for those things which are pleasing in his sight.

Your welcome letter of the 13th is to hand. Its contents rejoiced me. I do not recall whether I have mentioned in any of my previous letters a statement once made by a simple countryside woman: 'Growth in grace is like the growth of a cow's tail—the more it truly grows, the closer to the ground is it brought.' That is true. The more we grow spiritually the more out of love do we become with ourselves, and the lower place do we take before God. After upwards of twenty-five years in the Christian life, I can truthfully say that none but *God* would have borne with me all these years. The fact is that the more the blessed Spirit reveals to us and convicts us of the ocean of corruption which indwells us, ever casting up its mire and filth, and the more we are brought to mourn over our waywardness and wickedness, the better for the health of our souls. Yet that is flatly contradictory to the 'religion' of the day. You say, 'How some so-called children of God can maintain that they live without sin is far too much for me to understand'—1 John 1:8 explains it!

With reference to your problem presented by the Baptist minister asking you to 'lead the singing' in his church: First, let me ask you a question: Do you think that if the apostle Paul or John was preaching in Atlanta, to either saved or unsaved, he would have any 'choir' or any 'special' singing or music? I fully believe it was at this point that that which has most widely 'quenched' the Spirit was introduced. Thousands of services open with a thirty-minute sing-song instead of prayer! I am well aware of the fact that if the 'sing-song' were now abolished and a prayer-meeting substituted the people would not attend, for God will not be mocked with impunity. Again, modern hymnology has encouraged thousands of people to sing *lies*. Imagine 500 people—half of whom were at the baseball game on Saturday afternoon, and the movie in the evening—singing on the Sabbath, 'Oh, how I love Jesus'. How would the officers of that church regard the preacher if he said, 'Only truly born-again souls can sing this hymn truthfully, so will the unconverted please *not* join in singing it'? I know from sad experience. Such a preacher soon empties the church! Again, it opens the door wide for bobbed-haired, face-painted 'flappers' to show off in some solo or anthem where they can trill the high notes. And I am not a music-hater, but a trained musician, both vocally and instrumentally! But now, more directly, for your problem—as to whether or not the Baptist preacher's invitation may possibly be a call from God.

For your general guidance, I would point out that when God calls anyone to any service in his name (never say 'for him', as though you were doing him a favour or that *he* needed our assistance), he first equips him for that particular work. It is only Pharaoh (the Devil) who requires us to make bricks without supplying the necessary straw! Second, he gives him a natural aptitude for the work, as women have for teaching children, as authors have for literary labours, and as missionaries whom God calls have for acquiring foreign languages. Third, he gives him a desire and love for the work, so that his very heart and soul are in it. Hence, if any man (or woman) urges you to undertake in Christ's name any work or service for which you are not equipped, not capacitated, and for which you have no genuine love, you may be certain it is not of the Lord.

If the Lord has purposed you should marry he will equip you for the woman of his ordaining, fit her for you, and make you a real help the one to the other. But it is only right and fair to her that you should first learn by grace to rule yourself, before she submits to your rule or headship!

Yes, emphatically, one tenth of all the money a Christian man receives belongs absolutely to the Lord. I enclose my booklet on Tithing.

The law on capital punishment in this Christian era is not

(rightly) based on any statute given to the nation of Israel, but is grounded on the unaltered edict of Genesis 9:6! Many of the statutes given to the nation of Israel pertained to them only—such, for example, as the not eating of 'unclean' animals. Christ's precepts in the Sermon on the Mount apply only to Christians in their private or personal lives, and were never given to or for magistrates to execute from the Bench!

No fresh news to report. Thankful to say all is well with us. Many thanks for your kind gift.

With loving greetings,

Yours by God's abounding mercy,

Proverbs 2:1–5

18/THE SABBATH, EVANGELISM, AND SCOTLAND
Lowell Green

386 Great Western Road
Glasgow
Scotland
Sabbath-day, July 7, 1935

Our Dear Brother in Christ,

Greetings in the blessed name of him who declares, 'If any man think that he knoweth anything, he knoweth nothing yet as he ought to know' [1 *Cor* 8:2]. How this should humble us and remove pride far from us! How ignorant the wisest is! At best, we now 'see through a glass darkly'! It is not how much of the Scriptures we know with our heads, but how much of them is written on our hearts and is regulating and transforming our lives. It is at that point so many make a mistake; they suppose that if they have a clear intellectual grasp of divine truth and give a mental assent to the same, then all is well with them, whereas Christ says, 'If ye know these things, happy are ye if ye *do* them' [*John* 13:17]. O that by God's enablement we may be '*doers* of the word, and not hearers only, deceiving your (our) own selves' [*James* 1:22].

Hearty thanks for yours of June 23rd and its kind enclosure. Yes, it is indeed well for us to make Psalm 90:12 our daily prayer. By nature we are strangers to 'wisdom', for as the Word tells us, 'Foolishness is bound in the heart of a child'— born thus. Hence, we have to be 'taught' it, and as no man can impart 'wisdom' to us, we need to be divinely taught; and even that, not in a general way but '*so*' taught that we will truly 'apply our heart unto wisdom'. You know how things go in temporal affairs when a man really puts his 'heart' into it!

About the Sabbath: I am writing my Publisher in Swengel (for at the moment I do not have a copy on hand) to send you my booklets on *The Law and the Saint* and *The Christian Sabbath* —the latter is really a branch of the former, so kindly read *The Law* first. Both will need an attentive perusal. I think Bunyan's treatise was specially designed for the refutation of seventh-day sabbatarians.[1] Bunyan was a Puritan and not a Plymouth Brother. I may say that 'Puritan' is not a sectarian appellation (like 'Baptist' or 'Methodist'), but is generally accorded to all the godly during the seventeenth century. The Dark Ages (when Rome dominated) ran from about 600 A.D. till about 1500. Then came the Reformation from 1500 to 1550. Following the separation of the Reformers from Rome, the next two or three generations were granted even fuller light and grace, and from 1590 to 1650 a purer Christianity obtained than at any other period since the apostles. From 1650 onwards, things deteriorated, though not so noticeably till after 1700 A.D. Thus men like Owen, Bunyan, etc., who lived around 1650 are designated 'Puritans', because of the spiritual purity of their times. The name originally was sneeringly given them by their

[1] *Works* IV, 193 pp. Stebbing Edition.

enemies. The Plymouth Brethren originated about 1830, through J. N. Darby. For fifteen years I was misled by much in their writings, but after I began to study the Puritans, I soon discovered how far they were astray on almost every doctrine; and today I have no hesitation in saying that the writings of J.N.D.[1] and C.H.M.[2] are full of error, although in a very subtle form, which can only be detected by one having a deep and wide grasp of the truth.

Now, as to the expression 'The Lord's day', this is one of the titles of the Sabbath. It intimates that the change of day from the seventh to the first of the week is by Christ's authority, for 'Lord' always brings in the thought of authority. 'The Son of Man is Lord also of the sabbath' [*Mark* 2:28] was a strong hint that he was about to change the day. It is equally correct for us to term Sunday 'The Lord's day' or 'the Sabbath', but personally I believe we ought to use the latter in these days for the following reasons: (1) Because 'the Lord's day' has no clearly defined import in the minds of most people. So long as they go to church once or twice on that day, they appear to think they are free to use the remaining hours of it as they please. (2) Because the sabbath is now so generally repudiated—by the Plymouth Brethren and through the very wide influence they have exerted. When I say the Sabbath is now generally repudiated, I mean that the sabbatical character of the Lord's day is denied or disregarded—i.e. that on the Lord's day or sabbath *no* work is to be engaged in, other than works of mercy (tending stock or the sick, etc.) and works of necessity (kindling a fire if one would freeze without it, etc.). (3) Because, while 'the Lord's day' occurs only once in Scripture, the 'sabbath' is mentioned scores of times. That shows us where the emphasis should be placed. It is not wrong to speak of 'the Lord's day', but in my judgment it is much better to say 'the Sabbath-day' for the three reasons given; that is to say, 'the

[1] John Nelson Darby   [2] C. H. Mackintosh

Christian Sabbath' to distinguish it from the Jewish Sabbath. I trust I have expressed myself clearly on this point.

The pamphlet you enclosed, about the 'Gipsy Smith' meetings in Atlanta, is thoroughly typical and representative of what is now going on, everywhere, in the religious realm. It only shows what a dreadful state Christendom is now in! Could you imagine the apostle Paul, come to Atlanta to preach the gospel, allowing himself to be eulogized and magnified in such a fulsome manner? I notice the name of *Christ* is not mentioned once in this leaflet, while the preacher's name is mentioned sixteen times! The awful thing is that were you (or I) to open our mouth in protest we would be denounced as fault-finders, critics, those who can see no good in anything. The awful thing is that you could probably number on your fingers all those in the whole of Atlanta who saw anything radically wrong with this 'Campaign'. And the fearful thing is that, under emotional appeals (instead of conscience-searching) music, touching anecdotes, and death-bed stories, hundreds, perhaps thousands, will be moved to make their decision, sign the card, and be fatally deceived into thinking they are *saved*. As Christ says, they 'make him twofold more the child of hell' —on their way there before they heard the 'Gipsy', but now hopelessly doped, chloroformed, but still on their way there, yet thinking, saying, and singing 'I am on the way to heaven'. I personally heard the Gipsy over twenty-five years ago, and have read through a volume of his sermons. Of course he brings in just enough Scripture and says just sufficient concerning the cross of Christ to delude the superficial. How deeply thankful *you* should be that God, in sovereign grace, has opened your eyes! No, by no means, say nothing at all to Dr Hull—just drop out completely from the Institute and their 'tent'.

I regard all real and avowed followers of Dr. Bullinger as rank heretics. It is a basic error to repudiate the two Christian ordinances of baptism and the Lord's supper. But that error grows out of a deeper one, viz. their wild idea of 'rightly dividing the word of truth'. They are fundamentally unsound on the whole subject of 'Dispensationalism'; and ought to receive no support from real Christians.

Re Mrs. C. Cluhan, née Miss Elliott, first suffer me to point out that you get on to very dangerous ground when you attribute a Christian's doubts to the Devil. Often they are to be ascribed to the Holy Spirit withholding his comfort because he has been grieved! Further, I think you need to be more cautious and conservative when you say 'she has been a child of God for some years'. It is much safer to say, 'who seems to have given good evidence of being a child of God'. All is not gold that glitters. God's flock is a little one. No doubt some of Gipsy Smith's converts will experience a thorough outward reformation; quit swearing, movies, betting, and attend church regularly; and their Christian friends will be fully assured it was a 'genuine conversion'. But let a true servant of God come and preach election to them, and they will soon evidence the character of *goats*!

About the article you refer to, entitled 'Delusions Discovered', October 1933. My readers vary much in type. That article—I did not write it myself—was meant for some of my Plymouth Brethren readers who are so cocksure of their salvation, yet have no scriptural evidence to show for it. I suggest that your friend should make a careful study of my 'Assurance' articles in the same volume.

I verily believe that Evelyn is the girl God has appointed for you as wife. The only point I am exercised about is whether *his* time has arrived for you to be married, and that is largely to be ascertained through his providence, and whether you are now circumstanced so as to heed Genesis 2:24, and maintain her. No wife ought to earn her living while her husband is blessed with health. I am seeking to pray earnestly that you may be kept from running ahead of the Lord, and that he will grant you grace to wait *his* time.

Once more I must be very brief in giving you my general impression of spiritual conditions in Scotland. In general, they are much the same as elsewhere. I attended in all 30 services at the Free Presbyterians but with only one exception had no sense of God's presence, power, and blessing. They are very one-sided; on the solemn and gloomy side, afraid of joy. They never address or refer to God as 'Father', but always as 'the Most High'. Hardly any of them have any definite assurance. It is almost all *law* and scarcely any gospel or grace. They are fearfully sectarian. But I must stop now. Our united love and best wishes,

Yours by God's abounding mercy,

Romans 8:25
James 1:4

19/SATAN'S DEVICES
Lowell and Evelyn Green

386 Great Western Road
Glasgow
Scotland
29 September, 1935

My Dear Brother and Sister in Christ,

Greetings in the blessed name of him who exhorts and assures us, 'Resist the devil, and he will flee from you' [*James* 4:7]. Alas, many of the Lord's own people today are so ignorant of Satan's devices, that they cannot even recognize his approaches, still less resist them. Many suppose that his temptations are restricted to external baits which he sets before us, in his efforts to lead us into some outward sin. But far more often his attacks are internal, by means of suggestions to the mind. Especially is this the case where he strives to prejudice some Christian against a servant of Christ, whom God has used in blessing to his soul. There are none upon all the earth whom the great Enemy hates so bitterly as the faithful ministers of the Lord—and there are very few left now! He leaves no stone unturned to undermine their influence. Sometimes he will lyingly assail their moral character, as I think it is clear he did Paul's; or why should the apostle say 'For our exhortation was not of deceit, nor of uncleanness, nor in guile' [1 *Thess* 2:3], which is evidently what he had been falsely charged with. Sometimes he will attack their doctrine, charge them with heresy, and emphasize how much their teaching differs from that of all other preachers—can it be possible that all others are wrong, and they alone right? At other times he criticizes and condemns the counsel they give to souls along practical lines, and here he very often succeeds! He will whisper in the ear of those whom God's true servant is seeking to help—'That is none of his affair, he is interfering with what is none of his business; he is trying to tell you what to do in everything'. Alas, many heed these satanic suggestions, without realizing the source of them. I can tell you from sorrowful experience that I have lost more than one intimate Christian friend in the past in this very way. How thankful I was then to receive your letter of the eleventh! God knows that what I and Mrs. Pink[1] wrote to you and Evelyn in our last few letters was written solely with the desire to honour him and to help you. We were, and are, so desirous of seeing you start out right and enter into the Lord's best for you, and according to our limited light we sought to counsel according to the *Word*. You are much more than correspondents, with whom we exchange letters; we love you

---

[1] After the Greens married, the letters to Mrs Evelyn Green were normally written by Mrs Pink.

both in Christ. Yet love is faithful, or it ceases to be love. I trust that I can say in some measure, 'For I am jealous over you with godly jealousy: . . . But I fear, lest by any means, as the serpent beguiled Eve through his subtilty, so your minds should be corrupted [by his lies] from the simplicity that is in Christ' [2 *Cor* 11:2, 3].

It is indeed much to be thankful for that the Most High has been pleased to reveal to you the blessed truth of his sovereignty, and I trust he will now make just as clear to you the equally important, and equally hated truth of our relationship to his Law. I wish you would carefully re-read my article thereon in last year's *Studies*. As you read, and meditate thereon, jot down on a slip of paper any particular difficulties which occur to you, and any objections, or any passages which appear to be on the other side. Then, arrange them in definite form and send them to me, and I will endeavour with God's guidance to help you thereon. Cannot you see, dear Lowell, that if God be Sovereign, that is, King over all, he must have a rule or law by which he governs his subjects and which is the rule of their accountability? Again, is it not clear that if Christ has left us an *example* to follow, we must be 'under the Law' [1 *Cor* 9:21], for he most assuredly lived his life here under God's law, see Galatians 4:4 etc. The great mistake so many make is in supposing that grace and law are irreconcilable opposites—enemies: that is because they understand neither grace nor law! The key verse on grace is Romans 5:21, grace 'reigns through righteousness', and not by setting it aside. To repudiate the law is to 'turn the grace of our God into lasciviousness' [*Jude* 4].

We deeply appreciate the details you so kindly gave us of your marriage, and the snapshot you enclosed. I need hardly say that you have our very best wishes and prayers, that God may richly bless your union, make you a spiritual help the one to the other, and grant you all needed grace, wisdom, forbearance and prosperity.

I thank you in his name for the further kind gift, which I have applied to the *Studies*, as we do all gifts received by us, for since the death of my father, our own temporal needs are provided for. May the Lord reward you for it! I am happy to report that prospects for the Magazine have improved considerably during the last few weeks—all praise to him who has heard the cries of his children on our behalf. I trust that both of you rejoiced when you read the 'Welcome Tidings' in the July issue.

We are gradually making a few friends in Scotland. O that God may be pleased to make us a blessing to them! Thankful to say we are preserved in good health. Wishing you much happiness,

Yours by God's abounding mercy,

Psalm 119:132

20/CONDITIONS IN SCOTLAND
John C. Blackburn

386 Great Western Road
Glasgow
Scotland
Sabbath-day, August 25, 1935

Dear Brother,

Greetings in the blessed name of him who teaches his people to pray, 'Lord I believe; help thou mine unbelief' [*Mark* 9:24]. How well suited is this petition to those who are conscious of the present conflict between the 'flesh' and the 'spirit' [*Gal* 5:17]! None but the Lord himself can afford us any 'help' from the awful workings of unbelief, doubtings, carnal fears, murmurings, Thank God one day we will be done for ever with 'unbelief'.

Your very welcome letter of the 6th is to hand. Many thanks for its kind enclosure: may it be 'treasure' laid up for you in heaven. Yes, 'many months' have slipped by between your last communication and this, and I was the more disappointed that you failed to give me your findings on the three points I raised in my last—anent this age being the final one, and the Resurrection—to which you promised to give careful thought and study. We are grateful for your prayers: we need them—the path does not get easier: temptations to compromise and paying the price for refusing to do so! Moreover, we are finding it increasingly difficult to locate those who relish spiritual literature, until it now looks as though it will not be long until we may have to cease publishing through lack of really interested readers!

Our experiences here have been no happier than elsewhere the past seven years. A number of our readers assured us there would be a place for me among the Free Presbyterians—who broke away from The Free Church in 1893 because of its heterodoxy (Higher Criticism) and worldliness. We attended their local church here in Glasgow for a couple of months, and though the services were very lifeless the doctrine taught was sound. The pastor called on me to lead in public prayer several times. The sequel was very sad. At their annual 'Synod', held in Inverness the last week in May, the senior minister moved 'That their men be prohibited from calling on those of other denominations to lead in prayer or otherwise assist in their services'. The minister who seconded the motion said, 'We do not wish to hobnob with people of other denominations'. This appeared in the local newspapers. On his return, I called on the local pastor who confirmed the accuracy of the report and added 'We are a very exclusive people'. Yet they are very short of ministers, and had rather some of their pulpits be vacant (no service at all), than be filled by one (whose writings they profess to greatly admire) who cannot conscientiously 'join' them—refusing to use him as an occasional 'supply' or 'stop-gap'. So, as you say in the States, 'That's that'. We have not been back again to any more of their services, nor have I preached a single time this year. O what a state poor Christendom is in!

Here in Scotland it is either dead 'orthodoxy', with the presence and power of the Holy Spirit noticeably absent; or rank heterodoxy with the worldly in attendance. In comparing general conditions in Scotland with those obtaining in the U.S.A. account has to be taken of the Scottish temperament—slow, cautious, conservative; but politically, socially, morally and religiously things here are rapidly approximating to those obtaining in America. Rome has already made tremendous advances in the land of Knox.

Regretfully, I must say that I greatly fear I can be no use to you in locating the books you mentioned. During the war when there was a shortage of paper and the pulp from which it is made, the government bought up huge quantities of second-hand books at £12 per ton; and in consequence, a great many second-hand book shops went out of business. One can find nothing worthwhile today in the few that remain.

I note what you say about 'Adoption': have not I covered most of the ground in what I wrote on 'Regeneration', and earlier, on 'The New Birth'? If you think I did not, and if the manuscript you mentioned once differentiates sharply between 'Adoption' and 'Regeneration' and preserves that distinction throughout its discussion, I shall be obliged for the loan of it, and will give it a careful reading and return.

Am thankful to say we are kept in good health and trust you are too. With all good wishes,

Yours by God's abounding mercy,

21/DEEP THINGS OF GOD
John C. Blackburn

386 Great Western Road
Glasgow
Scotland
November 11, 1935

My Dear Brother in the Faith of God's elect:

Greetings in the ineffable name of Jehovah: may our hearts be filled with holy awe as we (most feebly!) endeavour to contemplate the grand mystery of the unity of his nature and the trinity of his persons: such I doubt not will occupy us much in heaven.

Yours of October 29 to hand. I greatly appreciate your kindness in sending me what you did: the two packages arrived this a.m. I hope to give each a careful reading, for I recognize that Dr. Girardeau was a real 'theologian'. You have indeed made me your debtor: kindly accept the enclosed $1 to defray postage—I feel I cannot do less. Later, I hope to send you some comments on this valuable literature anent 'Adoption'. I shall prayerfully endeavour to peruse the same with as open a mind as possible and I trust you will not be pained should I take exception to, or differ from, any of the positions taken by Dr. Girardeau. I fear this is likely, for I am a strong supra-lapsarian, and in my humble judgment, any one who is not firmly fixed there is bound to go astray in his subsequent thinking and postulates. I have not arrived at that conclusion hurriedly, in fact was not confirmed therein till after twenty years of continuous study, during which time I read more than one million pages of religious literature, a goodly proportion of which was 'theological'. After carefully reading Twisse, Thomas Goodwin (on Ephesians 11), John Gill, etc., and weighing closely the arguments used by those who differed, I am forced to conclude that there was an order to God's decrees or eternal counsels and that he first ordained the end, and then the means necessary to the securing of that end. God's grand end was the glorification of himself by the Mediator. To that end God (the Triune God) first predestinated that the Second Person should take a created nature, manhood, into union with himself so that this manhood in union with the Logos, should be his 'fellow', the 'delight' of his soul [1 *Pet* 1:20, *Is* 42:1, *Col* 1:15, each of which I believe, refers to the eternal decree to unite manhood to the person of the Logos]. Second, to the grand end that the Triune God should be glorified by the Mediator, God ordained that the God-man should be the Head of a people, family, church, taken into union with himself, which people he 'blessed with all spiritual blessings' (including 'adoption'—the status and place of 'sons') in the heavenlies in Christ [*Eph* 1:3]—which 'spiritual blessings' are, in part, enumerated in Ephesians 1:6. Third, God purposed the entrance of sin and the fall of his people in their natural 'head', to make way for the glorifying of himself by the redemptive work of Christ. The Church was given to Christ as his Bride and Body altogether apart from and (in the order of his 'counsels') before his foreview of sin, as Eve in her purity was given to Adam before his fall. Thus, Christ sustains a dual relation to the church: note the order in Ephesians 5:23— 'Christ is [first] the Head of the Church, and [second] he is the Saviour of the Body' . . .

With all good wishes

Yours by God's abounding mercy,

22/NOT DESPISING 'THE DAY OF SMALL THINGS'[1]

386 Great Western Road
Glasgow
Scotland
December, 1935

'For who hath despised the day of small things? for they shall rejoice' [*Zech* 4:10]. Three lines of thought are suggested by these words. First, in the history of the church there *are* periods which may justly be termed 'the day of small things'. Second, the temptation arises to *disparage* God's work at such times, because of its 'smallness'. Third, assurance is here given that despondency shall give place to gladness and they who lightly esteemed the lesser displays of God's gracious power shall be followed by those who 'rejoice'.

It was 'the day of small things' when the little remnant of Israel returned from their captivity, repaired the walls of Jerusalem, and built the house of God. The temple of Solomon far surpassed in splendour the one erected by Zerubbabel. As God said to the Jews through Haggai, 'Is it not in your eyes in comparison of it as nothing?' [2:3]; yea, when many of the ancient men saw its foundation laid, they 'wept with a loud voice' [*Ezra* 3:12]. Nevertheless, the Lord *was* working, and therefore did he issue this challenge to their hearts '*Who* hath *despised* the day of small things?' Even the minor displays of God's power and the lesser blessings of his mercy are not to be disparaged.

Our lot is also cast in a 'day of small things'. When present spiritual conditions are compared with those of fifty years ago, the difference is most marked: in the number of faithful

[1] The annual letter from *Studies in the Scriptures*, 1935.

preachers of the Truth, in the number of homes where the family altar is maintained, in the demand for really helpful literature. The *cause* for this contrast may be looked for in two directions. First, in the *sovereignty* of God, for he does not act uniformly. Some seasons enjoy a much more bounteous supply of rain and sunshine than others: as it is in the natural realm, so it is in the spiritual. Second, the *unfaithfulness* of the Lord's people. Where light is given and it be not walked in, where great privileges are granted and there be no corresponding fruit, the Holy Spirit is grieved and quenched, and further blessings are withheld. *Both* of these factors explain the present situation.

Yet God *is* still working. In various places there are 'showers' of blessing, even though the 'former rains' be withheld. While there is much that calls for exercise of heart, humiliation of soul, and confession to God, yet there is no warrant for abject despair. The question asked in Zechariah 4:10 is a challenge, and perhaps a *rebuke* to some of us: shall we 'despise' what God is now doing because it be a 'day of *small* things?' If God is still maintaining a testimony for the Truth, and a few souls are being blessed here and there, that is proof he has not entirely abandoned Christendom. Moreover, a Divine promise is coupled with the challenge: O for faith to lay hold of it—'for they *shall* rejoice'. Brighter days are ahead. Christ will yet crush the Serpent's head beneath his feet!

It is in the spirit of Zechariah 4:10 that we desire grace from on high to carry on this work. The past year has been one of severe testing. Hitherto the Lord has moved many of the readers to send in their contributions early in the year (which, for the magazine, begins December 1), so that by the end of March only a smaller amount was needed each month to meet expenses. But this year it was otherwise: all through it has been a case of 'from hand to mouth', and sometimes the meal in the barrel was almost—though not quite!—exhausted. Yet to the praise of our faithful God be it recorded, that he *has* graciously moved different ones to send in something each week (£4–20 dollars—is needed every week, the year round), so that only one bill is before us, and before that is due we fully expect to have sufficient on hand to more than meet it.

We have also been much exercised over the smallness of our circulation. As each year passes, we are finding it harder and harder to locate those who really relish spiritual literature. The popular demand is for that which is light and superficial, or for that which is startling and sensational. Many prefer anecdotes, brief articles, or comments upon the latest doings of Hitler and Mussolini. Few are willing to *study* that which calls for concentration of mind, and fewer still articles which search the conscience. But we dare not lower the standard. Many of our older readers have been called Home, and it is very difficult to find new ones to replace them. Very few *co-operate* with us in seeking to make this magazine known to fellow-Christians. How many would *really* be sorry if we were obliged to cease publishing for lack of support? How many are endeavouring to *prevent* this by their efforts?

We have now to remove from our list several hundred names, to whom we have sent *Studies* this year: those whose names were given us by friends, or who applied personally themselves; but who have manifested no appreciation of its contents—owing to the smallness of our circulation, it costs 3/6 (90 cents) to send to each person for a year. *Where* are we going to find new readers to fill their places? Unless we do so in the near future, we will not have sufficient names on our book to carry on! We know that some readers have done their best to interest others; but there are many quite indifferent. If half of our readers could introduce us to just one Christian who would welcome this Magazine, it would be a great relief to our minds. Show your copies to those likely to be interested: not to those looking for something for nothing, but those hungry for soul food. Do please carefully consider this appeal.

Another thing which has deeply concerned the editor is that no doors have been opened for oral ministry. From the human side, two things place us at a great disadvantage. First, having lived almost all our Christian life in the U.S.A. and Australia, we are virtually unknown in Great Britain. Second, not being prepared to 'join' any denomination or sect makes most of the 'churches' unwilling to use us. Do any of our readers know of any undenominational cause or 'independent' church, anywhere in Great Britain, where a man of Truth would be welcome, or any 'Mission', conducted on scriptural lines, where there would be openings for Bible Conference addresses? Our preaching is along the same lines as our magazine articles. Some readers have a wide acquaintance and may know of suitable openings, and God may use them to give us contact with places that would welcome an uncompromising and soul-edifying message. Please pray over this, *and write us.*

The days are evil, the need is great, many of Christ's sheep are being starved, very little real gospel is now preached. Soon our race will be run: what little time is yet left us, we desire to be used wholly for the Lord, and to be made a blessing to his people. Many 'churches' and places we could not enter because of their heterodoxy and worldliness. How are we to make contact with *sound* ones for a week's special meetings? Cannot *you* be of assistance here? If not, will you please definitely supplicate the throne of grace on our behalf? By the mercy of God we have both been preserved from all illness through another year. Earnestly soliciting your prayers, with hearty Christian greetings and with all good wishes, we remain,

Yours by God's abounding mercy,

23/RECEIVING THE WORD: PRACTICAL COUNSEL
Lowell and Evelyn Green

386 Great Western Road
Glasgow
Scotland
Sabbath-day, December 8, 1935

Our beloved Brother and Sister in Christ,

Greetings in the blessed name of him who bids us 'receive with meekness the engrafted word' [*James* 1:21]. Our first duty is not to understand God's Word, but to *receive* it. It is at that point so many fail: they are not prepared to receive what Scripture says—on election, on baptism, on separation from Christ-dishonouring 'churches', on the Law, and on many other things—until they think they have understood it. That is because of *pride* (little as they may realize it). Scripture must be made to bow to their intellect, rather than their intellect to the Scripture! But more especially, it is because of *self-will;* what Scripture says crosses their (sinful) desires and conflicts with their views. Hence, James 1:21 says 'receive with meekness'. Though often confounded with it, meekness is an entirely different grace from humility. Meekness is pliability of spirit, mouldableness of heart, being clay in the hands of the Potter.

Your very welcome letter of November 19 has come to hand. I am happy to know you are persevering in your study of the Law in relation to the Christian. You are labouring at a great disadvantage, for not only is the whole trend of present-day thought and teaching on the subject opposed to the truth, (and it is always difficult to row against the current), but the whole of your 'old man' *hates* the Law [*Rom* 8:7], though you may be but dimly conscious of the fact, and it will seek and use every advantage to prejudice you against the truth. I am therefore happy to find that (as you say) 'James 1:5, 6 has been much on our hearts of late'. Continue [*Col* 4:2] pleading it before God daily. I may say that the word 'wisdom' has a wider meaning and more comprehensive significance in James, than it has in other epistles; he uses the term almost synonymously with godliness, piety, and grace, in its utmost latitude. Compare James 3:17 for the force of the term! It is only as that heavenly 'wisdom' is communicated that your heart will be 'easily entreated' by the Law!

I suggest that you take as your starting-point—'receiving' and suffering nothing to shake you, 'under the Law' [1 *Cor* 9:21]. Probably your mind at once recalls the 'not under the law' of Romans 6:14. Therein your meekness is at once put to the test! Pride and self-will would say, 'Well, Romans 6:14 comes first, and 1 Corinthians 9:21 must yield to it.' Humility and meekness would say, 'I may not understand how the two statements can be made to agree, but as there cannot be any contradictions in God's Word, I "receive" them both as *true*; I refuse to pit one against the other.' Taking the two declarations together, there must be a sense in which the Christian is *not* under the Law, and there must be a sense in which he is under the Law. What are those senses? Answer: he is not under the curse of the Law, but he is under the rule of the Law. Again, he is not under the Law as in the hands of God the Judge, but he is under the Law in the hands of Jesus the Mediator; hence the force of 'under the law to Christ' in 1 Corinthians 9:21! Please do not hesitate to mention any particular difficulties or special verses on the subject which puzzle you.

Many thanks for your further kind offering to the Lord's work in our unworthy hands: may he richly bless you for the same! You will rejoice to learn that, by the great goodness of our faithful God, we had a record November so far as gifts for the magazine were concerned, and that after paying every bill promptly we closed the year on the 30th with a nice credit balance. Hallelujah! We serve a great God, and he is greatly to be praised. The new year has also opened very promisingly, though we are still much exercised over our small list of names for 1936. Please continue in prayer about this.

I note the prospect of your moving, to occupy half of a bungalow. In my heart I am secretly hoping the Lord may have intervened, for I rather fear such an arrangement could hardly prove satisfactory to you. There is an old saying that 'no house is large enough for two families', and I have seen the wisdom of it exemplified in quite a few cases. However, the Lord takes various ways and means of reminding us that 'this is not our rest'. He loves us too well to suffer us to become satisfied with any earthly conditions; as soon as we do, he generally stirs up our nest! Thorns and briers are often needed to detach our hearts from the things of this world. You will probably recall these sentences in days to come! But no matter what wilderness buffetings and roughings you may be called on to endure, my earnest prayer is that you may be kept from doubting either God's love or wisdom.

May I utter a word of warning against acquiring many books. Life is short and time is valuable. The Puritans were very wordy, and one often has to read many pages to get only one or two helpful thoughts. A few really helpful books thoroughly assimilated count for far more than skimming through many ordinary books.

I would like to write more, but this is my seventh letter today, and I have still another I must answer. May the Lord graciously work in each of us that which is well-pleasing in *his* sight, and grant us all needed wisdom to receive and follow *his* Holy Word no matter what the cost to the flesh. With our united love and every good wish,

Yours by God's abounding mercy,

Ezekiel 9:4

24/GLORY AND PRAYER
Lowell and Evelyn Green

31 Colbourne Road
Hove 2
Sussex
Sabbath-day, May 24, 1936

Beloved in the Lord,

Greetings in the holy and blessed name of him who declares, 'But we all, with open face, beholding as in a glass the glory of the Lord, are changed into the same image from glory to glory, as by the Spirit of the Lord' [2 *Cor* 3:18]. The 'glass' in which the 'glory of the Lord' is revealed, is, of course, the Scriptures: but the Scriptures are divided into two Testaments, the respective contents of which may be summed up as 'the Law' and 'the Gospel'. The 'glory of the Lord' (cf. John 1:14 etc.) has reference to his moral attributes, for we are never conformed to his incommunicable perfections—his omnipotence, omniscience, omnipresence, immutability. Now it is in the 'glass' of his Law that God's holiness and righteousness are exhibited; while in the 'glass' of his gospel we see his grace and mercy. As by the Spirit's enabling operations we are 'beholding' this 'glory of the Lord', we are 'changed into the same image', that is, answering principles and affections are communicated to and wrought in our hearts—i.e., there is a love for holiness and righteousness, and a desire to exercise grace and mercy in dealing with our fellows; all of which is only another way of saying that God 'writes his laws on our hearts', or stamps his 'image' upon us [*Col* 3:10].

The 'from glory to glory' denotes that this divine work of moral transformation (the Greek word for 'changed' here is the same one used of Christ in his 'transfiguration', Matthew

17:2) is a gradual and progressive one—cf. the 'more and more' of Proverbs 4:18! The first degree of this 'change' is wrought in us at our regeneration. The second degree of it is effected during our 'practical' sanctification. The third and last degree occurs at our glorification. As someone has said, 'Won't we be beautiful when God has finished with us!' That which exercises and so often distresses the sincere Christian is that, as he honestly examines himself, he can discover so very little evidence that he *is* being 'changed into the same image'. But, my dear Lowell and Evelyn, if God permitted us to see through the clouds of dust and dirt which the constant exercise of indwelling sin stirs up within us, and discern, beneath, his 'workmanship' which is secretly going on in our souls ('renewed day by day'—2 Corinthians 4:16), would we not, in our present condition, be filled with *pride*? Verily, 'It is the glory of God to conceal a thing: but the honour of kings is to search out a matter' [*Prov* 25:2]. We, as 'kings' [*Rev* 1:6], are to 'examine' ourselves [2 *Cor* 13:5], and seek to make sure that 'the root of the matter' [*Job* 19:28] *is* within us. Remember, dear friends, that as his countenance reflected the glory of the One with whom he had spoken face to face for forty days, 'Moses wist not [knew not] that the skin of his face shone' [*Ex* 34:29]! *He* was unconscious of the 'change' wrought in him, but others perceived it!

Your ever-welcome letter of the 10th is to hand. Yes, Luke 18:1 is very blessed and searching. In reality, Lowell, I believe that you *pray* much more, or I should say, much more frequently than you realize, or is registered in your memory afterwards. I mean brief ejaculations for divine help under pressure. Prayer is the spontaneous unburdening of the heart to God, and a cry for divine aid. This is a vastly different thing from 'saying' prayers or going through a 'religious' exercise such as millions of the unregenerate do daily. *Don't* attempt to pray by the clock! Be quite artless and simple and remember that a groan from the heart reaches the ear of God as quickly and truly as does a song of praise! Almost all of the so-called praying in Christendom today is as non-spiritual as the belief accompanying it is non-scriptural! And each of us has been more contaminated by this state of things than we realize. In like manner, almost all that is written today on the subject of prayer is not only worthless, but positively injurious.

Yes, I am thankful to say that our new living quarters are confirming our first impressions. It is truly a 'peaceable habitation'!

Thank you for answering my query about our Sister's 1928 volume: may it please the Lord to make its contents a real blessing to Mrs. Foley!

We are so glad to hear that the Lord has dealt graciously with Evelyn, and have sought to bring her case before the throne of grace.

Thank you in his name for your further kind gift to the *Studies*. You will be pleased to hear that the Lord continues to send in funds freely. I trust you spend a part of each Sabbath in reading the magazine. May the Lord be very gracious to both of you to supply 'all your need'.

With our united Christian love,

25/PRACTICAL CONSIDERATIONS
Lowell and Evelyn Green

> 31 Colbourne Road
> Hove 2
> Sussex
> Sabbath-day, March 14, 1937

Our dear fellow-members of the Body of Christ,

Greetings in the blessed name of him whose Word records, 'and he found a ship going to Tarshish' [*Jonah* 1:3]. What a strange sentence to begin my letter with! Is it? Is it not a part of Holy Writ, and so 'written for our learning'? Ponder it a moment, in view of its context, and see what line of thought, what valuable lesson it inculcates. The Lord had bidden Jonah 'Go to Nineveh' [*v* 2], but that was a most distasteful commission to the prophet's state of mind. He rebelled and determined to flee to Tarshish. But that involved a voyage, and ships were not so plentiful in those days, nor did they sail according to our modern schedules! However, when Jonah reached the dock, here was a ship to hand, all ready to sail, going to the very place on which he had set his mind. How providential! How gracious of the Lord! Of course he must be displeased at Jonah's unwillingness to go to Nineveh; but then he is very merciful and remembers we are dust! So in his longsuffering goodness, he now 'undertook' for his servant, showed himself 'strong on his behalf', yes, 'opened up the way' for Jonah to go to Tarshish!

How very easy for Jonah so to conclude! How natural for him so to interpret this providential interposition on his behalf! There was the ship ready to carry him, the captain making no demur when he proffered himself as a passenger! Surely this was God's provision for him! But was it? *No*, far from it! 'Be not deceived: God is not mocked' with impunity: when we 'mock' him, he often 'mocks' us in return. True, 'he opened the way' for Jonah, but the sequel was disastrous, and only sovereign grace prevented his death! And this particular incident is recorded for our learning. But why have I called your attention to it? Ah, dear friends, cannot you apply to your own case the principle which underlies it? The providential interposition of God is *not* a rule for us to walk by. The *Word* is given us for that purpose! Oftentimes God, as it were, sets before us an open door, *not* as intimation he would have us enter it, but to *test* our hearts! How often the wish is father to the thought! How readily we jump to a conclusion that such and such a thing is 'the Lord's will for me', when that conclusion coincides with our secret desires!

What I have written thus far has been suggested (not as a rebuke, but for you carefully to weigh and keep in mind) by what you said of a possible new home. First, let me say that neither the nearness nor the remoteness of Christ's return is a rule to regulate us in the ordering of our temporal affairs. It is parallel with the possibility of death. Spiritual preparedness is the great matter! With regard to temporal things, while youth and health is ours, our responsibility is to act accordingly; for example, not to refuse to marry because death may strike us down within the next few days. On the other hand, our house should be 'set in order'; for instance, I hope you have already made a will! Second, let me say very emphatically that I think you would act very unwisely if you purchased any property. I know of more than one or two brethren in Christ in the U.S.A. who heartily wish they had never saddled themselves with property. Take only one angle of it. Suppose you bought a house, it being exactly suited to your needs, and two years hence you are transferred to New York or Los Angeles! It is one thing to buy property, and quite another to *sell*! Third, I can quite understand your desire to remove from where you now are; from the first, my letters have intimated that no house is large enough for two families! But I do hope you will not 'jump out of the frying pan into the fire', as they say here.

You need to pray for 'good judgment'. A thing needs considering from many angles. Don't make haste. I have no advice to offer, but would indicate general principles. God has so ordered things that there is a law of compensation governing all things here. Everything earthly has certain advantages, and certain disadvantages—gains and losses. This is true of marriage; true if you have children or are without any; true whether you be an employer or an employee. So of the location of a residence; whether it be in the city or in the country; there are certain drawbacks whichever you select. In the country, the air is purer, there is more quietness and privacy. On the other hand, time is wasted going to and from work, and buying a cheap car has its disadvantages as well as advantages! A wife is more exposed and has less protection against tramps etc. Shopping is a bigger problem, and if goods are 'delivered' beyond the city limits you have to pay more for them, directly or indirectly! Fewer friends call on you; the doctor is harder to reach in case of sickness, especially at night-time, and so on. All these points have to be considered.

I thank you in his name for the enclosed gift: please convey my thanks to Evelyn's father for his share therein.

I thought I had answered briefly your query about reading newspapers, etc. Much depends on your motive, and what it is you dwell on. Anything necessary to keep you posted on business matters or world events is legitimate; but shun all political speeches, murder cases, and such like.

Yes, there is much in the experiences of Elijah which contains valuable instruction for us: if I am spared, and it is the Lord's pleasure for *Studies* to continue, I intend to follow David's Life with a briefer series on 'The Life of Elijah', and then on 'Elisha'.

I am so glad to hear of your father's spiritual progress. If you have not already purchased, and decide to get Manton, I believe I can secure his 22 volumes for much less than $30.

Your little one is now approaching her most attractive stage, and much wisdom, and patience, will be required to strike the happy medium between laxity and undue severity.

Am thankful to say that all is well with us. The Lord be very gracious to you and yours, lead you not into temptation, but deliver you from evil. With our united love,

Yours by God's abounding mercy,

26/DISCOVERING THE WILL OF GOD
Lowell and Evelyn Green

31 Colbourne Road
Hove 2
Sussex
Sabbath–day, September 19, 1937

My Dear Brother and Sister in Christ,

Greetings in the holy and blessed name of him who declares, 'Many are the afflictions of the righteous, but the Lord delivereth him out of them all, [Ps 34:19]. On occasions these 'afflictions' are in the form of anguish over the discovery of our inward corruptions; at other times over the low state of Christ's cause in this world, or our sympathy for some of his suffering members; at still others they are occasioned by our adverse circumstances. Some of these 'afflictions' are part of the entail of our fall in Adam, many of them are caused by our own folly, some of them are due to our faithfulness to Christ; but out of them all the Lord ultimately delivers us.

No, dear brother, I do not have more time than formerly for

letter-writing. As each year passes, the composing of many
articles which are read by many of the same readers requires
more and more of my time. I am very far from thinking that
you are ungrateful for the efforts I have made in my letters to
be of some help to you, yet I realize today more fully than
ever, that neither you nor any other of the younger ones whom
I love in the Lord can walk by my faith or profit from my
experiences. Each one has to live and learn for himself.
General principles of conduct I may set forth, but the application of them to the details of your life will have to be worked
out by yourself. If I write fewer and shorter letters to you in
the future, it will *not* be because I have lost, or have less,
interest in you both, or because I consider that my efforts have
resulted in no fruit in your lives, but because I have already
given you the substance of the best of what God has given me,
and because I shall be seeking (D.V.) to pass on the same to
others.

It is indeed a splendid thing when we really desire God's will,
and nothing else, to rule our lives, yet, as I have several times
suggested in recent articles, desiring God's 'will' is a very vague
and often a most confusing expression, and the all-important
question of *how* his will is to be known, generally leaves one
in a state of utter perplexity. Let me illustrate. Am I to purchase
a new suit of clothes for this winter? My natural and fleshly
inclinations say 'yes'; my spiritual instincts raise the question,
'Would it be for God's glory?' I am now undecided. I tell
myself I want God's 'will' in the matter, and not my own. Yes,
but how is his will to be ascertained? There is no specific verse
of Scripture on the point; nor will the state of my finances
supply an infallible answer. True, if my pocket be empty, that
settles the matter, for I must never run into debt. But suppose
I have $100 in hand? Well, that in itself does not justify me
buying the suit.

What then am I to do? Wait on God and ask him to make

his 'will' clear? But what good would that do? We are only brought back to our first query of 'How is his will to be ascertained by me?' Perhaps you reply, 'Suppose after such praying, I was unexpectedly to receive a gift of $50 or a rise in salary, would not that be clear intimation that God wanted me to buy the suit, and was here providing the money for it?' Not necessarily: he might thereby be testing you! No, the better way would be to ask him to give you good judgment, and act on it. God holds us responsible to use our common sense, carefully to weigh pros and cons, to learn lessons from past experiences when we acted hastily and rashly, to profit from observing the mistakes others have made. It is always God's will for us to use our best judgment—after praying him to give us such.

Now for the example in hand: Do I really need the suit? Would I by purchasing it make it impossible to buy other things which I or my family need more, or are more important? What am I likely to lose (my appearance at business etc.) if I don't buy the suit? These, and such like questions, must be carefully considered and answered. Thus, I change the vague question of 'Is it God's will for me to buy the suit?' to, 'Is it right, necessary, wise to do so?' I would suggest that you carefully re-read the articles on 'Divine Guidance' in 1934 *Studies*, pages 212, 260, 281, and in January 1935. And here I must stop, as several other important and difficult letters require my attention; a young preacher in Chicago earnestly desiring help to prepare experimental sermons; another from a missionary in Salvador begging a solution to some nasty problems in his 'field', and so on. The Lord be very gracious to you and yours. Our united love and best wishes—as ever,

Yours by God's abounding mercy,

27/CHRISTIAN DUTIES
Lowell and Evelyn Green

31 Colbourne Road
Hove 2
Sussex
Sabbath-day, February 27, 1938

Beloved friends in Christ,

Greetings in the holy and blessed name of him who commands, 'Whatsoever thy hand findeth to do, do it with thy might' [*Eccles* 9:10] which means, put your very best into it, do it as unto the Lord himself, whether it be manual labour, work in the office, or domestic duties.

Your welcome letter of the 13th is to hand. I am glad to know that your new employer is strict and requires accuracy, and I regard this as a gracious providential provision from God, furnishing needed discipline. Scripture says, 'It is good that a man bear the yoke in his youth.' Slackness and carelessness are inexcusable in a child of God. He should ever present a model and example of conscientiousness, painstaking care, and exactness. Prayerfully ponder Ephesians 6:5-8; Titus 2:9, 10; 1 Peter 2:18-20, and remember that these exhortations are as binding upon you as the Ten Commandments. It is obedience to these precepts which God requires from you, and not going around speaking to people about their souls. I know from experience of both that the former is a much harder task than the latter. What I am here pressing upon you is practical Christianity! Unless your reading of the *Studies* and my letters have, under God, made you a better workman in the office, more conscientious and reliable, they have profited you little indeed. And until you faithfully discharge your responsibilities in the office, it is most unlikely that God will ever call you to minister from a pulpit. I believe you may glorify him more where you now are, than in any sphere of 'Christian service'. May the Lord grant you a hearing ear!

I note from your letter that you have read and discussed with your father and uncle my booklets on *The Law* and *The Sabbath*, though you do not state how conclusive (or inconclusive) you found them. I trust you are now more definitely established on these most important subjects. Not only all the leading Puritans, but Jonathan Edwards and Spurgeon taught that the moral law is the Christian's rule of life!

No, the *Treasury of the Old and New Testaments* does not duplicate exactly the sermons by Spurgeon found in the 20 volumes published by Funk and Wagnell, though many of the same occur in both. Permit me to say again, lovingly but earnestly, the money you spend on books ought to be placed in a savings account, and not touched for anything except serious illness. It is a tempting of God to be in steady employment and not saving something each month! You are disobeying God if you do not lay by for a rainy day. I feel very strongly on this point. I gave the same scriptural counsel to others twenty years ago, who were then of the age you now are, and today they bitterly regret their disregarding of it.

Hearty thanks for the kind enclosure: please express my thanks to your father, father-in-law, and Mrs ——.

With Christian love and every good wish,

Yours by God's rich mercy,

P.S. Thanks very much for the stamps: the boys are delighted, and would value a few of South and Central American States if any come your way.[1]

[1] Pink had begun to collect stamps for some youngsters. Later in 1939, through his wife's encouragement, he became a stamp-collector himself. She was intrigued to discover how philately had helped George V and Theodore Roosevelt to relax, and hoped it would have the same effect on her husband!

28/THE OUTBREAK OF WAR
Lowell and Evelyn Green

31 Colbourne Road
Hove 2
Sussex
September 10, 1939

Beloved in Christ,

Greetings in the blessed name of him who assures us, 'My times are in thy hand' [Ps 31:15]. When faith is exercised upon that truth what comfort is ours; how the heart is stabilized !

Your good letter of August 16 (written from Hiram) came duly to hand; please accept our hearty thanks for the kind enclosure. May the Lord truly bless both givers and gifts ! I had expected to write to you last Lord's day, but conditions were such that we were not in a suitable mood. Just after 11 a.m. the nation was informed, 'We are now at war with Germany'. Less than an hour later we received the first air-raid warning, conveyed by loud sirens lasting two minutes. All round the coast we have air-planes patrolling, on the watch for advancing enemy planes, and as soon as they see any of them they flash the news inland. As soon as the warning sirens sound, everyone on the streets must at once take shelter indoors. Those already at home retire to the room specially fitted-up for protection against poison-gas. We have been living for the past three years in upstairs rooms, rented already furnished. Our land-ladies have fixed up the living-room downstairs in their part of the house, which is large enough to accommodate us as well for a limited time. This prepared room has been rendered air-tight so that no air from the outside can enter it. This is a precaution in case the enemy should drop bombs filled with poison-gas.

The general expectation is, however, that if an attacking squadron of German air-planes were to penetrate our defences they would use incendiary bombs, filled with high explosives and inflammable matter. Against that form of attack civilians are helpless, unless they prepare deep 'dug-outs' in their back gardens and strengthen these with concrete sides and roofs. A few have made this provision, but we have not, and we do not expect to. The Government has furnished us all with gas masks, which we have to carry in a box slung over our shoulders whenever we leave home to shop, etc. The air-raid warning last Sabbath morning came as quite a shock, for we did not even know that war had been declared. However, I am thankful to say we were both kept quite calm, though rendered uneasy because our landladies were away at church. It turned out that the alarm was quite unnecessary and an hour later the 'all clear' signal was sounded by the sirens—it was stated that a 'friendly' plane had been sighted by our observers which at first they were unable to identify. Two days later we went through the same experience, but with the same harmless sequel. We are thus kept in a state of more or less tension all the time, for we have no means of knowing what hour day or night we may be bombed. Yet there is *no* panic or 'jitters' among the people.

At the moment I can make no definite statement as to the future of the magazine. I have written to my printer, but he has not yet replied. Our desire is to continue publishing, and if God is pleased to spare our lives (as he assuredly will if he has any further service for us down here), I fully expect we shall do so, for another year at least. I hope to make a definite statement in the November or December *Studies* upon the matter. We look for a regular mail service to be maintained between this country and the U.S.A., though sailings will probably be less frequent and thus letters take longer to come and go. It will be quite in order for you to transmit money by international money order, but please have the orders made out to us at Hove and *not* Brighton. If your post office at East Point will not do this, please send from Atlanta. Do not be unduly worried about us; we are quite safe in the Lord's hands— Proverbs 1:33 ! Please make a point of praying daily for God's saints in Germany !

From the contacts I have had with those who handle a lending library, I think they are more bother than they are worth, and I would not advise you to saddle yourself with one. Thank you very much for the promise to send me the stamps if Mrs C. gives some to you. We have noted the new address of your father.

Am thankful to say this leaves us both quite well in every way except that I have a head cold. We have abundant cause to praise the Lord. May he continue his favours to each of us and keep us faithful to the end !

With our united love,

Yours by God's great mercy,

29/WAR DEVELOPMENTS
Lowell and Evelyn Green

31 Colbourne Road
Hove 2
Sussex
October 8, 1939

Beloved in Christ,

Greetings in him whose holy word declares, 'My son, if thou be surety for thy friend, if thou hast stricken thy hand with a stranger, thou art snared' [*Prov* 6:1, 2]. 'A man void of understanding striketh hands [the ancient custom when sealing or confirming an agreement], and becometh surety' [*Prov* 17:18].

'He that is surety for a stranger shall smart for it: and he that hateth suretiship is sure' [*Prov* 11:15]. I know not why I should be led to call your attention to these divine warnings, but they are the passages which came before me after waiting on the Lord. But this I can say, that in my varied experience I have personally known more than one dear brother in Christ who has been made to 'smart' severely for his folly (however well-meant his intention) in having gone surety for someone. And therefore I would lovingly and most earnestly counsel you, *Never*, under any circumstances, go on anyone's 'note'—no, not a close kinsman's! And this reminds me that once or twice during the past year or two (the last time when you mentioned a rise in your salary) I have counselled you on another matter which you have not acknowledged in your replies; namely, the matter of your living strictly within your income and saving a portion of it every month! Permit me to call your attention to a Scripture on the point: 'The children ought not to lay up for the parents, but the parents for the children' [2 *Cor* 12:14]. Though its meaning there is a spiritual one, yet the apostle could not have made this spiritual application unless the general principle was literal. Are you, dear brother, 'laying up' for your little one? God says you *ought* to!

Your welcome letter of September 10 came safely to hand three or four days ago. Letters passing between the U.S.A. and England now take almost twice as long in transit as they did before the war began. Please accept my heartfelt gratitude for the money order enclosed, and convey my thanks to those who had a part in it. I have duly entered the orders for the 1939 bound volumes, but at the moment of writing I am unable to give any promise about them. We are hoping we shall be able to get them bound and to make a statement about them in the December issue. Much business is considerably disorganized, but probably conditions will improve as the whole nation becomes adjusted on a 'war basis'.

There is little news for me to report; probably you in the States know much more about what is now going on in Europe than we do, for all news here is heavily censored. My own impression is that the entrance of Russia into the conflict has considerably complicated matters all round, and at present both sides seem to be marking time.[1] I would appreciate it if you would kindly let me know, briefly: What seems to be the general impression among those you are acquainted with as to the justice and wisdom of Great Britain and France declaring war on Germany upon her invasion of Poland? Second, what was the reaction to Soviet Russia's entry and the pact between Germany and Russia? Third, to what extent does the German element within the U.S.A. appear to be influencing public opinion? Are they ashamed of Nazi-ism or do they vindicate it? Fourth, what is the general idea about the length of the war? Is it likely to be a short or a long one? I am already posted on the repeal of the Neutrality Law, so you need not refer to it.

Whatever happens our own duty is quite clear; to continue publishing the *Studies* so long as God makes this possible and shows this is his will for us.

Thank you very much for the stamps you so kindly enclosed: they will afford me several hours of relaxation. Are they the ones you mentioned in your previous letter of August 16, in which you said 'Sister Currins has promised to give me a number which Brother Currins had saved for a granddaughter, who had lost all interest in them'?

We are comforted by the knowledge that you are remembering us daily at the throne of grace. I am thankful to say that all is well with us, and sincerely trust the same is true of you and yours. With our united love and every good wish,

Yours by God's great mercy,

---

[1] During 1939 Russia invaded Poland and attacked Finland. Poland was partitioned between Germany and Russia.

30/JUDGMENT ON THE HOUSE OF GOD
Lowell and Evelyn Green

> 31 Colbourne Road
> Hove 2
> Sussex
> Sabbath-day, December 3, 1939

Beloved ones in Christ,

Greetings in the blessed name of him whose holy Word declares, 'For the time is come that judgment must begin at the house of God: and if it first begin at us, what shall be the end of them that obey not the gospel of God?' [1 *Pet* 4:17]. 'Because they received not the love of the truth, . . . for this cause God shall send them strong delusion, that they should believe a lie' [2 *Thess* 2:10, 11]. These two passages have been much on my mind of late, and I believe they explain (account for) to a large extent what is now taking place on the earth. Judgment began at the 'house of God' in a pronounced manner some fifty years ago: seen (1) in the death of God's faithful servants (like Spurgeon), and others not being raised up to take their places; (2) in the banishing of God's *law* from the pulpit; (3) in the withdrawal of the Spirit's power and blessing; (4) in the marked decrease of genuine conversions. And today we are living in a world from which God is more and more withdrawing his restraining hand, giving up all nations to a spirit of madness. As truth has been muzzled in the pulpit, we must not look for it in the senate, the business house, or on the streets. A policy of unfaithfulness, temporising and compromising has been followed in the churches: ordination vows and articles of faith have been treated as scraps of paper, and such fables as evolution and the progress of man have supplanted the truth. Then why should we be surprised that so much which appears in the newspapers is untrustworthy? The public crave the unreal and the sensational, and accordingly the press caters to the public demands. What the outcome will be, what the future holds, no man can foresee.

Your good letter of November 5 is safely to hand. Thanks for having the last money order made out to Hove. Glad to hear Mrs. Currew changed her mind about the library. Yes, I have read and much enjoyed Flavel's *Fountain of Life*. His best book is on *Divine Providence*. He was one of the Puritans. Glad to hear the news about your parents. So pleased to know my opening paragraph of October 8 was a timely one; I felt very definitely led to write it. If spared for 1940 I wish both of you would read through Proverbs once each month (D.V.), a chapter a day. There are 31 chapters in it. Thank you for writing so fully in response to what I said about saving something each month. What I said (in a former letter) about not putting all your eggs in one basket, was because money invested in Government securities is safer than in any business concern.

Hearty thanks also for your kind trouble in replying to my queries about U.S.A. opinions. I consider Hitler, Stalin, Mussolini and the Japs equally menacing and dangerous. Hearty thanks too for the stamps you so kindly enclosed: I was particularly glad to get the three $1 ones, and would appreciate any more which may come your way; though those I would now like best are of the current series above 5c.

Am thankful to say all is well with us. With our united love and every good wish,

Yours by God's great mercy,

31/PATIENCE, CHILD TRAINING, CONTENTMENT
Lowell and Evelyn Green

31 Colbourne Road
Hove 2
Sussex
April 14, 1940

Dear ones in Christ,

Greetings in the blessed name of him whose holy Word
declares, 'The strength of Israel [what a title!] will not lie nor
repent [change his mind], for *he* is not a man that he should
repent' [1 *Sam* 15:29]. In these days when the most solemn
engagements and treaties are regarded as 'scraps of paper', and
when there are so very few whose word is their bond, how
comforting to know that we have to do with One who is
absolutely reliable, faithful and immutable! The prevailing
perfidy of men should make us esteem and value more highly
the integrity of 'him that cannot lie'.

Your good letter of March 24 came safely to hand. Thus
far, in spite of so many ships having been sunk, not a single
letter intended for the magazine or for us personally (so far as
we know), or any literature or letter mailed by us, has failed
to reach its 'desired haven'. Nothing is too great and nothing
is too small to commit into the hands of the Lord. We thank
you heartily for cashing the cheque I forwarded to you and
for your kindness in adding to it a gift of $5 from yourselves.
I may say I have felt led to use one dollar of your gift to send
a 1939 bound volume to a preacher who has taken the *Studies*
for years, and who wanted this bound volume but was
financially unable to purchase one.

With reference to patience, we need to distinguish sharply
between the *natural virtue*—what is termed patience among

men, which is largely a matter of temperament and health (the state of our nerves)—and the *spiritual grace* of patience. In the Scriptures patience is looked at as both a passive and an active grace. From the passive viewpoint patience is a meekly submitting to the sovereign dispensations of God so that we fret not and murmur not against them. From the active viewpoint patience is steadfastness or perseverance, so that we faint not and quit not because of the difficulties and trials of the way. If you will turn to your concordance and carefully ponder each passage where patience is mentioned, I think you will find full confirmation of the distinction I have drawn, though I have never seen anything on it in the writing of others. For example, the active side is seen in, 'Let us run with patience the race that is set before us'.

Yes, much wisdom and grace from above is needed in the training of children. Broadly speaking the two main things to aim at are, first, the pleasing of God therein, rather than yielding to the counsels and desires of relatives and friends! Second, the preserving of a proper balance between laxity and severity, sentimentality and cruelty. A child must be disciplined and taught it cannot have its own way in everything. The parent stands to the child in the place of God, and as he is to be feared (held in awe and reverence) as well as loved, the father should endeavour to promote both in his child.

Personally I believe it is altogether wrong for a child of God to enter into any financial commitment which binds him for years ahead. He must remain 'the Lord's freeman'—free to pull up his stakes at any time. God's people of old dwelt in 'tents'—which could be removed at short notice. You know not what God may call you to do five years hence, and in the New Testament saints are viewed as 'strangers and pilgrims'. Don't encumber yourself with any property. 'Having food and raiment [not 'property'] let us be therewith content'.

Monday morning:

Thank you for placing on your envelope the stamps you did and for enclosing the list issued by the Post Office, which I am herewith returning. I have ticked off those I already have. You mention: 'Am sending some other stamps you may not at present have'. There were none inside your letter when it arrived here. May I suggest that you please do not use one of the philatelic labels ('please cancel lightly') on the outside of your envelope when you are enclosing other stamps inside; it presents a temptation to dishonest Post Office employees interested in stamp collecting to steam open the envelope and take out stamps within. I am particularly interested in the new series of authors, poets, etc., so kindly save any you may get on letters. I want some for my young friends.

Thankful to say all is well with us. With our united love and best wishes,

Yours by divine mercy,

32/FROM HOVE TO THE HEBRIDES
Lowell and Evelyn Green

Scotland
Sabbath-day, October 6, 1940

Our beloved friends,

Greetings in the blessed name of him who 'hath done all things well'. Quite suddenly and unexpectedly, on September 20, the Lord made it very plain he would have us move from Hove, where rest, either day or night, had become virtually impossible. He knew our frames and graciously remembered we were dust. An old friend renewed his kind invitation (I had twice refused him) for us to come to them. It meant a long and hazardous journey of 750 miles, but the Lord removed all fear. I had to reduce my library and mailed to you a number of books I felt would be useful.

We left Hove early on the morning of September 24. First to London, where we had to cross the city by taxi from one railway station to another. While in the station there was a short air-raid and one bomb fell near, but we were unharmed. Then a 500-mile train trip to Glasgow, but the Lord granted full journeying mercies, though we arrived there late at night. We stayed a week with very dear friends and had a most refreshing time both spiritually and physically. It was a real oasis in the desert. There was a brief raid one night and we heard a few bombs, but there was no damage in our immediate vicinity. Next, a 170-mile rail journey to the north-west of Scotland and then a twelve-hour trip across the sea to the Island of North Uist (in the Outer Hebrides), which we reached safely without sighting any submarine. Finally an hour's journey by motor car across the Island at 1 a.m. and then we reached our 'desired haven', where all is peaceful and quiet. In a few days, D.V., we hope to move on to the Isle of Lewis and sojourn there, with friends, as long as the war lasts—isolated. We shall, D.V., carry on with the magazine. Hope to give you a permanent address in our next—in about two weeks' time—but felt we should send this now to let you know that, by the faithfulness and goodness of our gracious God, all is well with us. Have many others to write, so excuse more.

Warmest love,

33/MEEKNESS, TRAVEL, DUTY TO THE STATE
Lowell and Evelyn Green

> 27 Lewis Street
> Stornoway
> Isle of Lewis
> Scotland
> Sabbath-day, October 26, 1940

Beloved friends in Christ Jesus our Lord,

Greetings in the precious name of him who bids us, 'Take my yoke upon you and learn of me, for I am meek and lowly in heart' [*Matt* 11:29]. These words have been much on my mind of late. O that I may give better heed to them! By nature we are like 'the wild ass's colt', and therefore 'unaccustomed to the yoke' [*Jer* 31:18]—thoroughly intractable. What a marvel that God has not cast into hell such self-willed and rebellious creatures!

We can only be united to Christ in a practical way by taking his 'yoke' upon us, which denotes complete submission to his will and subjection to his authority, in order to be ruled by him. Not until we have voluntarily assumed his yoke ('take my yoke'—it is not 'laid upon' us!) can we experimentally learn of him. And what is it that we most need to be taught? How to obtain such wisdom that we shall be able to understand all mysteries? How to do such great things in his name that we shall become objects of wonderment? How to become so successful in his service that we shall secure the place of 'pre-eminence' among our brethren? No, *no*, nothing like that! Then what is it, blessed Lord, which I so much need to learn of thee? This: 'for I am *meek* and *lowly* in heart'.

Meekness is the opposite of self-assertiveness, it is pliability and gentleness, being clay (unresisting!) in the hands of the

Potter. Lowliness is the opposite of self-importance and self-esteem; it is humility, self-effacement. The 'meekness' of Christ appeared in his readiness to become incarnate, to be made 'in the form of a servant', to be 'made under the law'. His 'lowliness' appeared in his manger-cradle, his submitting to the ordinance of baptism (to the wonderment of his baptizer!), his washing the feet of his disciples. Alas, how little have I really 'learned of *him*', for there is still so very much of self-will and self-seeking still left in me!

These are some of the thoughts which I sought to embody in several articles which I wrote and Mrs. Pink typed (for next year's *Studies*, D.V.) while we were at Bayhead in North Uist, and I thought I would pass them on to you while they were fresh in my mind.

We went by motor car last Monday afternoon the 16 miles from Bayhead to Lochmaddy (the small port of embarkation) and spent a pleasant and, I trust, profitable evening there with a Christian couple, going aboard our steamer an hour and a half after midnight. We were due to sail at 5 a.m. but the sea was so rough that the captain did not deem it wise to sail till after 6 a.m. We had a very stormy crossing and I had a bad time of it, but arrived safely at port just after 10 a.m. We spent the day with friends and left at 5.30 p.m. by bus and arrived at Stornoway at 8 p.m. We received a most hearty welcome from the Presbyterian minister and his wife and we spent the night in their home. Next day she took us to the place where she had secured two furnished rooms for us, in a godly home, since when, right up to last night, we have been busy unpacking and getting things in order. There are a number of God's people here and I am sure we are going to be very happy. All is quiet and peaceful, and it was well worth an arduous and perilous journey to arrive here. How good the Lord has been to us!

And now a few lines in answer to your ever-welcome letter

of September 15. About your remarks on Psalm 139:18: no finite mind can 'count' God's thoughts concerning us. How grand to know that an endless eternity in his presence is before us! There is a balance to be aimed at between the objective and subjective aspects of the truth—looking to the Lord, looking within ourselves. The one should not preclude the other.

Now for your queries: Brighton and Hove adjoin each other, one city running into the other. The house in which we lived was only a quarter of a mile outside the borough of Brighton.

There is no doubt whatever in my mind that Great Britain did the right thing in declaring war on Germany. National righteousness required her to do nothing less. The question of an individual Christian's duty at such a time is not so easy to define, and many good and godly men differ about it. Undoubtedly the Christian can help most by prayer. Personally, I do not think a Christian should ever volunteer for military service. But suppose he be conscripted? Here, he must not defy the 'powers that be', yet he must not do anything inconsistent with his being a follower of 'the Lamb'. Personally, were I conscripted, I would lodge an appeal as a 'conscientious objector'—*not* from all forms of service but from that which required me to attempt to slay my fellow-beings. I would be quite willing to perform clerical or manual work for the Army. But each one must decide such matters for himself before the Lord.

We are hoping to have this year's *Studies* bound. As they will most likely (D.V.) be mailed out by my printer in Bath, it will help them if two or three are sent out in one package. Would you kindly ascertain within the next week or two (no need for hurry) how many of the 1940 bound volumes are likely to be required by you, your friends, Mrs. Foley and the members of her class; and whether we may mail them to you and her, instead of to each purchaser separately?

Though we are still feeling the effects of the very severe ordeals we have been through in the last four months, yet I am thankful to say we are both in fairly good health. May the Lord continue to show himself strong on behalf of each of us and perfect that which concerns us!

Yours by divine mercy,

34/WORKS 'COMMITTED', THOUGHTS 'ESTABLISHED'
Lowell and Evelyn Green

27 Lewis Street
Stornoway
Isle of Lewis
Scotland
Sabbath-day, January 12, 1941

Beloved ones in Christ,

Greetings in the blessed name of him whose holy Word declares, 'Commit thy works unto the Lord, and thy thoughts shall be established' [*Prov*. 16:3]. The duty and privilege which is here enjoined calls, first, for humility—a real sense of my insufficiency —for I shall never discharge it while I feel able to do the works or solve the problem by my own powers. Second, it calls for faith, as do all personal dealings with the Lord; faith in his readiness to hear me and willingness to undertake for me. Third, it calls for submission: a surrendering to his sovereignty, an unreserved willingness for him to have *his* way and order my lot as best pleases him. Fourth, it calls for the exercise of hope, which is a firm expectation that the Lord will show himself strong on my behalf and deliver me from the snare of the fowler. If I have thus 'committed' (or, as the margin puts it, 'rolled') my works unto (or upon) the Lord, then my 'thoughts shall be *established*', that is, my mind (concerning those works) shall be at rest. If my mind is not at rest, then it is clear that I have failed to commit my works unto the Lord: I have told him about them, but gone from him still carrying the burden. If my 'thoughts' thereon are not 'established', then I must seek the Lord afresh, with greater earnestness and definiteness (along the four lines mentioned above), seeking the enabling of the Spirit, pleading the merits and promises of Christ, and continuing until I have really cast my burden upon the Lord.

Your welcome letter of December 1–12 safely to hand, by the power and goodness of God. After reading the same, with its disquieting news of the possibility of your going out 'on to the road', Proverbs 16:3 came to my mind, and after looking above for guidance, what I have written on it is, I feel, to be the message for you. Personally I feel very strongly that it will *not* be for your spiritual good to go out as a salesman, and that you should beg the Lord to preserve you from that. Pray that he will either make your boss or sales manager willing for you to retain your present position, or that he will remove him and replace him with one more reasonable. Under no circumstances must you 'borrow money (from any one) to buy a car': 'Owe no man anything' forbids such a course. The subject of 'soul' and 'spirit' is too large for this letter.

Many thanks for the $9 money order and for permitting us to use $3 of it to defray postage on all the books I recently sent. I would like you to read the one by A. T. Pierson on *Character, Conduct and Culture*, (I think this is the title of it). Thankful to say we are well and happy in our new quarters.

With love and prayer,

Yours by divine mercy,

35/CHRIST, GOD'S PRUDENT SERVANT
Lowell and Evelyn Green

27 Lewis Street
Stornoway
Isle of Lewis
Scotland
Sabbath-day, July 6, 1941

Our dear Christian friends,

The Lord graciously brought safely through your wife's letter of April 22 with the money order for $17.01, to which Mrs. Pink will duly reply. Lowell's of May 8 has also arrived and is now before me. I am glad to learn that he is memorising verses of Isaiah 52 and 53 and then meditating on the same to and from work. He cannot be more profitably engaged.

As for Isaiah 52:13. First, I regard its opening 'Behold!' not only as a call for us to consider, to focus our gaze upon the one in view, but also and primarily as an exclamation, a note of wonderment. What an amazing spectacle to see the Maker of heaven and earth in the form of a servant! What an astonishing phenomenon that the Lord of glory should take on him such an office! '*Behold*!' wonder at it!

Second, take note of the *Father*'s owning of Christ in that lowly position. '*My* servant' he avows him! It was because the Messiah appeared in servant form that the Jews despised and rejected him. Apparently the holy angels themselves were nonplussed at such an incredible sight, for they received (I think, needed) the divine command, '*Let* [as though they were uncertain] *all* [the highest as well as the lowest!] the angels of God worship him', when God brought his 'first begotten into the world' [*Heb* 1:6]! How unspeakably blessed then to see the

Father himself testifying *his* approbation of the One who entered Bethlehem's manger, and bade the angels not be staggered at such a strange sight, but continue worshipping the second person in the Trinity, even though he now wore a menial's garb. Their obedience is recorded in Luke 2:12–14! 'Behold!—*my* servant' says the Father: and well may we be filled with wonderment and awe!

Third, 'My servant shall deal prudently' and here we must be much on our guard lest we interpret the words carnally. In the judgment of the world, to 'deal prudently' is to act tactfully, and nine times out of ten 'tact' is, with worldly people, merely a compromise of principle, taking the line of least resistance. Measured by worldly standards Christ acted very imprudently! He could have spared himself much trouble and suffering had he been 'less extreme', 'less unbending', and followed the religious tide of his day, had he been 'milder' in his denunciations of the Pharisees, had he withheld those aspects of the truth most distasteful to the natural man. Had he been 'more tactful', as our evil generation of professing Christians judges things, he would never have overthrown the tables of the money-changers in the temple and charged such unholy traffickers with making his Father's house a 'den of thieves'—for it was then he began to 'make so much (unnecessary) trouble for himself.' But from the spiritual viewpoint, from the angle of ever having the Father's glory in view, from the side of seeking the eternal good of souls, he did 'deal prudently', and none other than the Father bears witness to the fact! How different are God's thoughts from ours as to what 'prudence' really is! The remainder of the verse tells of the reward the Father bestowed on Christ for his willingness to become his 'servant' and for his faithfulness ('prudence') while discharging that office: the reward is described in Philippians 2:9–11.

A word now on the matter of contracting debts and the

course I have followed with the magazine. Our financial year closes on November 30; yet if readers in Australia (and we still have about 100 there) are to receive the January and February issues of the following year by say February (in normal times), I have to send the manuscript ('copy') to the printers for the January and February issues early in October, when of course I do not have the money in hand for them. Absolutely speaking that is not incurring a debt, for *if* the Lord did not send in sufficient money during the interval, I would pay the printer out of my own pocket rather than 'owe' them anything. Yet even if I were not in the financial position to do so, I should most probably follow the same course. But I most certainly would not order the March and April issues to be set up by the printers if I saw that the January and February issues were unlikely to be met by incoming donations. Take the other alternative: if I wait till I have the whole of the money in hand before asking the printers to begin their work, I should be acting by sight—there would be no room for the exercise of faith—and the publishing of the *Studies* is a 'work of faith' as well as a 'labour of love'. On the other hand, no matter how badly I needed a suit of clothes, I certainly would *not* order one till I had all the money to pay for it, and so far from trusting God, to act otherwise it would be tempting him.

You say, 'As to what constitutes debt, there seems to be a great diversity of opinion even among the more spiritual brethren.' Quite so, and the same would be the case with a dozen other matters. For your general guidance and help (on this and other things) I would recommend that you weigh the respective spirituality of their opinions. Which of their views seems most God-honouring? Which savours least of the world and carnal policy? You add, 'The present structure of this lopsided world makes the buying on credit terms more desirable in certain cases than to pay cash.' Even if that be so, has not God bidden his people, 'be *not* conformed to this world' [*Rom* 12:2]? The future 'well done' of our Lord rather than present ease or financial gain must be our aim; the pleasing of God, not of ourselves, or our friends, or brethren.

In the past I have seen the Lord more grievously dishonoured (in the end) by so-called 'faith' missions and churches than by those who made no such claim. The absence of any guaranteed 'salary'—accepting the free-will offerings of a group instead— is no proof at all that the 'pastor' is a man who looks to God alone for the supply of his needs, as quickly appears (in most cases) when the offerings fall off markedly!

You are correct in saying that if we look too hard we shall find our choicest idol has feet of clay, for 'in many things we all offend'. It is those who walk the closest with God who are most conscious of their sins, and I may add (in contrast to 'pharisees'), the readiest to acknowledge a (real) fault when it is pointed out to them. On the other hand, many a blemish (as the religious world now views things) is a virtue in the sight of God. Both of us have greatly enjoyed William Romaine's works for his magnifying Christ and seeking to get the believer occupied with him. Yet one also needs to read Owen in order to preserve the balance. Romaine is almost entirely the honey of the gospel; Owen brings in more of the salt. Romaine's ministry was a special one, needed particularly in his day to deliver the saints from legality and too much introspection.

From letters to hand last week it looks very much as though some at least of the March and April *Studies* were sunk en route to the U.S.A. If so I am sorry, for we have no duplicates to send. For several months now I have had much less liberty in praying for God to protect mails to and from U.S.A. It may be God intends to bring home more closely to the hearts of some of his children the real situation and the peril which is now getting nearer and nearer your shores. *His* will be done. From now on, those getting two issues of each copy, I intend to post singly, a week or so apart, to double the likelihood of at least one getting through. Am thankful to say all is well with us.

With Christian love,

Yours by divine mercy,

36/ATTENTION TO DETAIL
Lowell and Evelyn Green

27 Lewis Street
Stornoway
Isle of Lewis
Scotland
August 9, 1942

Our dear Christian friends,

'The scribes . . . walk in long robes' [*Luke* 20:46]. Christ 'laid aside his garments and took a towel and girded himself . . . and began to wash the disciples' feet' [*John* 13:4, 5]. What a striking contrast! It is the contrast between pride and ostentation on the one hand and humility and self-abnegation on the other. The scribes wished to be looked up to and made much of, but the incarnate Son 'made himself of no reputation' [*Phil* 2:7]. O to have more of his spirit! The 'flesh' in us loves display, and puffs up to self-importance; but when divine grace controls the heart our language is, 'He must increase, but I must decrease' [*John* 3:30].

The Lord has graciously brought safely through to us yours of June 19. I trust you will not be offended when I say that its opening paragraph on Psalm 27:14 rather disappoints me. After ten years' instruction from the *Studies* I had hoped you were acquiring the habit of noting carefully each detail in a verse, and not hurriedly and carelessly generalizing, as is the custom of so many in this rushing and superficial age. God's

Word is made up of words, each one of which is selected with divine discrimination and precision, and we cannot obtain even the surface and grammatical meaning of any verse except by noting and giving due weight to each term in it. When three or four consecutive verses are before us, often an important truth or lesson is acquired by our observing a change from 'we' to 'ye', or from the singular to the plural 'thou' to 'you' or 'them'; or the tense of the verb. After quoting Psalm 27:14 you say, 'Waiting on the Lord is one of the most difficult things we as believers are commanded to do'. There, dear friend, you are quite mistaken. Had you said, Waiting *for* the Lord is one of the most difficult things for a young believer, I would concur; but Psalm 27:14 speaks about waiting *on* the Lord, which is a totally different thing! Waiting on (upon) the Lord (see *Is* 40:31 etc.) describes an attitude of soul when we are engaged in true prayer, but waiting for the Lord is the exercise of patience while his answer tarries. There are certain lessons which we have to learn experimentally, under the Spirit, before we learn to 'wait patiently for him' [*Ps* 37:7b]. What those lessons are, is intimated in Psalm 37:1–7a, which I earnestly commend to your careful and prayerful attention. They are summed up in the words 'Fret not' [*v* 1], 'trust' [*v* 3], 'delight' [*v* 4], 'commit' [*v* 5], and 'rest' [*v* 7]! The order of those five things is divine and unalterable! We cannot obey *v* 7 till we have thoroughly heeded verses 1 to 6!

I note that you are remaining quietly at your present abode, and giving thought to what you feel needs doing to it. Your experiences in this should have taught you the need for going slow in making a move and for thoroughly investigating, examining and pondering the pros and cons of a thing, habitation or situation before definitely committing yourself. I am encouraged and pleased to find you writing, 'More and more it is apparent that in the so-called small things testimonies of believers are made or hurt—being punctual, being truthful, being courteous.' That is very true; large doors swing on little hinges! Apply the same principle to Bible study; it is the small words which often supply the key to the meaning of a passage. Apply it also to prayer: take the small things to God as well as the big ones.

I know of no satisfactory exposition of the Acts. Matthew Henry's comments are as good as any. The best of the smaller works on it is by Stiffler[1]—it may be among the books I mailed to you when I left Hove. Have you yet read the one by A. T. Pierson (on *Character*, *Conduct* etc.) that I recommended some time ago? I note that not many attend your class. A new broom sweeps well: the novelty soon wears off.

Glad to know you are still reading the *Studies*: the earlier ones as well as the present. Those on the Satisfaction of Christ are most important from a doctrinal viewpoint and the first value and use of Scripture is 'for doctrine' [2 *Tim* 3:16, 17]!

We thank you in the blessed name of our Master for your money order of $9.99 which the Lord graciously brought to us some days before your letter arrived. In future will you, briefly, if only on a separate scrap, kindly tell us in two separate letters from whom the money comes—in case one letter gets sunk.

Are young married men exempted so far from the Call-up in the U.S.A.? Or are they calling them up at intervals, a year at a time: first those born in '21 and then in '22 etc.? Instead of any revival, I warn you to be prepared for a steady and marked deterioration of character and conduct even among professing Christians!

Am thankful to say that all is well with us. We serve a great God and he is greatly to be praised. With Christian greetings and best wishes,

Yours by divine mercy,

[1] *An Introduction to the Study of the Acts of the Apostles*, J. M. Stiffler, English translation London 1894.

I earnestly hope you will never allow Anna to attend any Sunday School; responsibility of her religious training rest solely on you two.

37/ON FINDING READERS OF SPIRITUAL LITERATURE
John B. Culver[1]

> 27 Lewis Street
> Stornoway
> Isle of Lewis
> Scotland
> February 24, 1943

Dear Christian friend,

Greetings in him who moves his people to pray, 'So teach us to number our days that we may apply our hearts unto wisdom' [Ps 90:12]. O that we may be enabled to offer this petition sincerely, understandingly, and expectantly!

I thank you in my Master's name for yours of January 19 and the money order which has come safely to hand: may he graciously return it to you again in spiritual blessing.

My reaction to such letters as yours is twofold: gratitude that God has brought us into touch with another who relishes spiritual literature, and sorrow that the circulation of our magazine is so very restricted—now less than one thousand. The most noticeable decline in the last five years has been among our U.S.A. readers, yet during the twenty-one years of its life, more than half that time it was actually published in the U.S.A.

[1] J. B. Culver corresponded with Pink from 1942 until Pink's death. He was, at the time of this letter, a member of the First Presbyterian Church, Princeton, New Jersey, U.S.A.

We greatly appreciate your kindly efforts to secure new readers for us, but I wonder if they are being directed along the *most likely* channels. Long experience has shown that nineteen times out of twenty the *Studies* are unacceptable to theological professors, preachers and missionaries, unless someone makes them a present of the same, and then it is doubtful if they do more than glance over them. You are likely to have more success in locating those who are hungering for spiritual food among the laity—simple souls, in the background.

We are so short of readers I am entering you for an extra copy of this year's issue (D.V.). I suggest you give them out two at a time to different ones, preferably to young people (in their twenties or thirties) residing in rural districts.

All being well, will send you one of the 1942 bound volumes in about a month's time.

The works you have procured by Jonathan Edwards and John Owen are most excellent and should last you a couple of years. Don't hunt around for others until you have thoroughly absorbed these. One book read is worth more to you than a dozen on your shelves unread, and one book read slowly, meditated upon and assimilated is worth twenty skimmed through hurriedly. Many buy good books, go through them quickly 'to see what is in them', promising themselves a more careful perusal later on, but few fulfil their intention. Moreover to read rapidly and superficially destroys a person's power of concentration—that is why they remember so little! But enough: the Lord grant you wisdom and patience.

With all good wishes,

Yours by Divine Mercy,

38/ADVICE ON READING AND FEEDING

Lowell and Evelyn Green

29 Lewis Street
Stornoway
Isle of Lewis
Scotland
October 22, 1944

My dear Christian friends,

Greetings in the blessed name of him who records, 'But he giveth more grace' [*Jas* 4:6]. And what a good thing for us that he does! For if the regenerate were left to themselves, and all the operations of grace in them were suspended, they would never have a holy desire, think a godly thought, nor perform a commendable deed. O to be made increasingly sensible of our deep need of 'more grace'! Solemn is the warning that follows: 'Wherefore he saith, God resisteth the proud'. Pride is what closes the heart from receiving 'more grace'. A sense of self-sufficiency, a complacency over present attainments, is what chokes the channel of blessing. O to be made more conscious of the puffings up of pride, that we may resist its first workings! Encouraging is the concluding clause of the verse: 'but giveth grace unto the humble'. For humility we should daily pray. After humility we should earnestly seek, and if we would be successful in our quest, then we must heed Christ's injunction, 'Take my yoke upon you and learn of me.'

Yours of September 10 is safely to hand. Yes, my reading has been quite extensive, yet equally discriminating, for I have had much more time available for it than you. Yet I have devoted ten or probably twenty times as many hours to one or two authors as I have to fifty others put together! The same rule has governed me in this as did my hearing of preachers before I entered the ministry. Occasionally I attended the services of various men, but I was to be found much more frequently in one particular place, and that was where I received most profit for my soul. The writer who helps me the most is the one I devote the most time to. And thus it should be with you. If you get more real profit from perusing Pierson, Newton, or any other man, than you do from the *Studies*, then it is obviously the part of wisdom for you to give him the preference.

But before turning from this point I will name some of the criteria by which I measure the helpfulness of a preacher or writer to my own soul. The one who most profits me is the man whose ministry brings most of the awe of a holy and sovereign God on my heart, who discovers to me my sinfulness and failures, who conveys most light on the path of duty, who makes Christ most precious to me, who encourages me to press forward along the narrow way.

I charitably assume that the brief account of how you spent your vacation time gives but a very one-sided picture, and would fain hope you were at least equally diligent in looking after the interests of your souls. The real needs of our bodies are very few and simple, but we live in an age when many, especially in the U.S.A., make a 'god' of their belly. Except for a few green cooking apples and some rhubarb, we have had no fresh fruit for four years—no eating apples, pears, peaches, plums, bananas or berries. Yet our health is just as good now as ever it was! Two thirds of people's physical ills are brought on by over-eating and by mixing too many things. Here, too—like books and preachers—it is better to confine ourselves to a few staple articles of diet and use others sparingly! However, most have to learn by painful experience, preferring to follow their own ideas or blindly to imitate their fellows, and then discount the way of wisdom when their digestive organs are worn out.

The war is too controversial a subject for me to take up. I therefore refrain, except to say, 'Those who live longest will see the most.' The great war for the Christian to be concerned about is to be 'striving against sin' [*Heb* 12:4] in himself, and to 'fight the good fight of faith'. May the Lord teach us both more effectually to take 'the whole armour of God'!

With best wishes,

Yours by divine mercy,

39/ON PSALM 37:25
Miss Clara Brown[1]

29 Lewis Street
Stornoway
Isle of Lewis
Scotland
August 6, 1945

Dear Christian friend,

Greetings in him who says, 'If ye love me, keep my commandments' [*John* 14:15]. Nothing pleases and honours him so much as an obedient walk. How we need to pray 'Make me to go in the path of thy commandments' [*Psalm* 119:35].

With regard to Psalm 37:25. That is not a Divine promise but a personal observation which David made, and was inspired to record. *Never* are 'the righteous' forsaken: that is a rule without exception. *Seldom* do 'their seed beg bread': yet such *may* occur through their dissipation or idleness. With Psalm 37:25 should be compared such passages as Proverbs

[1] Miss Clara Brown of Florida, U.S.A., received *Studies in the Scriptures* for many years, and this letter contains Pink's reply to a query on the relationship of Psalm 37:25 to Luke 16:19–22, a problem which puzzled her for some years. Miss Brown has been responsible for the indexes in a number of Pink's works.

19:15; 20:4; 23:21! Such a calamity occurs so rarely that David had never seen a case, nor, so far as I know (and I have been a Christian nearly 40 years and have travelled completely around the world), have I. But Spurgeon said *he* had met several such. The 'beggar' of Luke 16:20–22 is not alone: see Mark 10:46, John 9:8, Acts 3:2, yet observe that in each case Scripture is silent about their ancestry; we know not whether their parents were 'righteous' and therefore should not assume they were. I have never written on the subject, but the above gives you whatever little light I have on it. I am always glad to receive questions on the Word, particularly those relating to the spiritual life, which have a practical value. I am anxious to be of service to exercised and perplexed souls.

With best wishes,

Yours by divine mercy,

40/AGAINST FEARING THE FUTURE
Lowell Green

29 Lewis Street
Stornoway
Isle of Lewis
Scotland
July 4, 1946

My dear friend,

Greetings in the blessed name of him who says, 'I would have you wise unto that which is good, and simple [uninformed— the opposite of wise] concerning evil' [*Rom* 16:19]. I wonder whether you have ever pondered those words, or inquired what the last clause implies and signifies. Personally, I feel it is an injunction which the Lord's people especially need to take to heart today. I am convinced they are greatly the losers by not doing so. In various ways our subtle enemy is seeking to occupy the saints with *evil*, and a great many preachers are aiding him in his work! Satan (and note well, the very next verse, Romans 16:20, begins with 'And', and then refers directly to 'Satan'!) is persuading many professing Christians it is their duty to be 'well posted' concerning current events, and induces them to waste much time upon secular literature and the radio. The 'signs of the times' men hysterically rake over all the evil they can find in the moral, social and political spheres and all the disconcerting doings in the international situation, all of which is contrary to Romans 16:19! And what good is accomplished thereby? Your worrying over the Kremlin, my concern about the Vatican, will effect nothing, neither retarding nor hastening the return of Christ by a single moment! No; but it will do *us* much harm: it will get our minds off spiritual things, disturb our peace, and make us fearful about what may soon come to pass! You have no responsibility for the running of this world, nor have I, nor does God require us to take the burden of it on our shoulders. *He* is ruling it, and there you may, and should *rest*. Your business, my business, is to be 'wise unto that which is *good*'. Let the devil's victims concern themselves with 'evil'. I trust you will re-read this—for I have written it under very heavy pressure of work, jealous of your spiritual interest—and turn it into daily prayer, for grace to *heed* it.

Your welcome letter of June 16 is to hand. Glad to hear you are memorising the opening verses of John 15; meditate frequently on each separate clause [*Ps* 1:2]. Hearty thanks for your very kind trouble and care. Once more you have placed me in your debt; volume three of Gill and one and two by Hawker have arrived in first-class condition. The valuation I placed on them was what I paid for them ten and twenty years ago. There are no secondhand book shops in Lewis and I now know of none in Britain; nearly all were destroyed in the bombings, and others have gone out of business because there is no demand for religious literature. A few really worth-while books thoroughly mastered and absorbed mean more to any man than a hundred superficially skimmed through.

Thankful to say all is well with us. With every good wish,

Yours by divine mercy,

Phil. 4:8 !

41/FORTY YEARS OF 'SOWING SEED'[1]

29 Lewis Street
Stornoway
Isle of Lewis
Scotland
December, 1948

'In the morning sow thy seed, and in the evening withhold not thine hand: for thou knowest not whether shall prosper, either this or that, or whether they both shall be alike good' [*Eccles* 11:6]. We have now entered upon what must be at least the beginning of 'the evening' of our life, for forty years have passed since the editor preached his first sermon. It was on the words 'For I am not ashamed of the gospel of Christ,' etc. [*Rom* 1:16], and to a congregation of over seven hundred people. Though it was not the first time we had spoken in public, yet it was quite an ordeal, especially as it was in our home-town—Nottingham. Since then, without any break, it has been our holy privilege, yet solemn responsibility, to sow the good seed, either orally or by the pen—the latter exclusively the last twelve years. Let the preacher observe that in the verse

[1] From *Studies in the Scriptures*, part of the annual letter for 1948.

with which we have opened it is not 'sow the seed,' but '*thy* seed'—that which we have, by grace, made our own, and verified by personal experience. *That* enables us to sow it with greater confidence, and often to better effect!

The discriminating hearer (and reader) can usually perceive whether the message is spoken from the heart or mechanically delivered like a gramophone; whether its author can say 'that which we have seen with our eyes, which *we* have looked upon, and our hands have handled of the Word of life ... declare we unto you' [1 *John* 1:1-3], or whether he be merely discussing something with which he has only a theoretical acquaintance. The figure of 'sowing seed' is a very suggestive one, among other things implying the exercise of *faith*; for to outward sight, so far as immediate results are concerned, it seems to be love's labour lost. For the same reason, it is an act of *hope*, performed with the expectation of a future yield. So it should ever be with the servant of God. After making sure he has a message from the Lord, and has first taken it unto and preached it to himself, he is to deliver the same in humble dependence upon his Master, and in the unshakable assurance that his Word will not return unto him void, but shall indeed accomplish that which he pleases.

'Thou knowest not whether shall prosper, either this or that, or whether they both shall be alike good.' Sometimes the servant of God is permitted to see fruits from his labours at an early date; at others he may toil all through a long night and take nothing. That may be ascribed to the sovereignty of God, though we are persuaded that 'according to your faith be it unto you' has not a little to do with it—'without faith it is impossible to please him' applies as much to preaching as to anything else. Sometimes a message upon which extra pains were taken, and which was delivered with unusual earnestness and liberty, appears to be lost on the air; while another which seemed far more commonplace is made a definite blessing to souls—which may be God's way of humbling the pride of his servant. In our experience with this magazine we have been particularly favoured by God, for during the course of the year scarcely an article appears but some write in to say it has been blessed to them—even the one on 'Counsels re Marriage' in the August issue was found especially timely by one reader about to wed—though when inserting it we knew that not.

Though this year has not been without testings and anxieties —for as Spurgeon well said, 'Joy and trial go hand in hand'— yet it has been a most encouraging one. An increasing number are kindly making this written ministry a matter of more definite prayer. *That* should be the chief recourse of all God's people in these evil days. The Lord changes not, and nothing is too hard for him. We greatly fear that conditions both in the churches and in the world will still further deteriorate, and that the spiritual and moral darkness upon Christendom will become denser. Yet, while that is a cause for grief and exercise of heart, it is no reason why we should panic or lose hope. God is our refuge and strength, a very present help in trouble. Therefore we should not fear 'though the earth be removed [the most stable forms of government], and though the mountains be carried into the midst of the sea [kings and emperors deposed]; . . . The Lord of hosts is with us; the God of Jacob is our refuge'; and he will maintain a testimony unto himself and make provision for his own unto the end.

During 1948 several old friends, both personal and of this magazine, have been called Home. On the other hand we have good reason to believe that more than one of our readers who were 'church members' have passed from death unto life while taking unto themselves some of the more searching parts of our articles; while others have been influenced to withdraw from places where error is taught, going forth unto Christ outside the apostate camp. The number of our ministerial readers is being maintained, and we feel increasingly desirous of seeking to help them and strengthen their hands—especially the younger ones. Though we had to drop well over two hundred from our 1947 mailing list (and shall have to do the same this time!), the Lord graciously gave us new ones to take their places, and some fifty more for 'good measure'. The smallness of its circulation is still our acutest problem. Had it not been that more than one hundred sent an annual donation which permits us to mail them an extra copy, we had been obliged to cease publishing years ago.

Prayer for us, for God's blessing on this magazine, and an increased circulation is earnestly solicited.

With Christian greetings,

Yours by divine mercy,

42/DELIGHTING IN THE LORD
A. V. Gilbey[1]

29 Lewis Street
Stornoway
Isle of Lewis
Scotland
February 9, 1949

My dear Friend,

Greetings in him who says, 'Delight thyself also in the Lord, and he shall give thee the desires of thine heart' [*Ps* 37:4] 'Also', in addition to the 'trust' of *v* 3, which ever precedes 'delight'. What is it to 'delight' one's self in him? Not only for faith to fix itself and feed upon his glorious attributes (joying in his grace, faithfulness etc.) but also to submit to his authority, finding my pleasure in those things that please him—compare

[1] A member of Westminster Chapel, London.

Proverbs 3:13, John 13:17 ('happy'). What is the relation between the second half of the verse and first? This: the more I am in subjection to God, delighting in his will (precepts), the more spiritual will my desire be!

I have been unusually crowded of late (I am thankful to say), and was unable to do more in reply to your welcome letter of January 17 than acknowledge receipt of the April issue. Exactly 20 were sent me! My Printers recently made another mistake: sending two of each of January and February to over 100 who were due only one (which did not include you), leaving me short.

Re Dr Lloyd-Jones on 1 John 1:7-9: I agree it is 'unscriptural' to speak of us 'putting our sins under the blood of Christ', yet it is not anti-scriptural: that is to say, although that expression is not in the Bible, it is not contrary to its teachings. It is a matter of terms. I simply meant pleading the blood when confessing our sins. It reminds me of a controversy when some criticized that hymn 'I lay my sins on Jesus'—quoting Isaiah 53:6. Yet in effect I do 'lay my sins on Christ' when I confess my sins to him.

Glad to hear you find it helpful to meditate on Psalm 119 verse by verse. Keep it up—along lines indicated in my first paragraph above. Sorry to hear of your wife's indisposition, and trust she will soon be 'in her usual', as they say in these parts. Am grateful for your prayers.

With every good wish,

Yours by divine mercy,

43/REST
A. V. Gilbey

29 Lewis Street
Stornoway
Isle of Lewis
Scotland
January 10, 1951

Dear Christian Friend,

Greetings in hom whose Word declares, 'In returning and rest shall ye be saved [from a physical breakdown, for example], in quietness and confidence shall be your strength'. Alas that so often it has to be added 'and ye would not' [*Is* 30:15].

Those are words to which the attention of God's children needs directing today, for the hectic spirit which characterises the world, has largely pervaded the churches, until its members are like Martha 'cumbered [weighted down] with much serving'. Many of them at work all day and rushing around to one meeting or another most week nights, so that they have no leisure for relaxation and quiet communion with God; and instead of the Sabbath being a *rest* day, with many it is almost the most strenuous one of the week. The result is that thousands of them are nervous wrecks by the time mid-life is reached! It is nothing but the restless energy of the flesh diverted into religious channels, which, so far from pleasing God, dishonours him. His people need to heed the word, 'Come ye yourselves apart into a desert [secluded] place, and rest awhile' [*Mark* 6:31].

Hearty thanks for yours of the 14th. I have delayed replying until such time as you would have returned from the U.S.A. where the tempo of life is even madder than what obtains in Britain. We much appreciate the three new names and trust the Lord will graciously bless the *Studies* to each of them.

I am sorry to say that I cannot pray over religious films for I do not believe that such are according to the revealed will of God. 'The weapons of our warfare are not carnal, but spiritual' [2 *Cor* 10:4]. We cannot improve upon God's methods—real prayer will accomplish far more than worldly devices for attracting the young.

With all good wishes

Yours by divine mercy,

44/GLORYING IN THE LORD[1]

29 Lewis Street
Stornoway
Isle of Lewis
Scotland
December, 1951

'He that glorieth, let him glory in the Lord' [1 *Cor* 1:31]. That is a proposition which ought to be perfectly obvious, for we have nothing good, either natural or spiritual, but what we have received from him; therefore the praise is due entirely unto him. But how humbling to realize that such a self-evident statement occurs each time in the form of an exhortation, and that addressed not to men at large but to the people of God! How it indicates what a vile nature still clings to the saint, since he needs to be warned against self-congratulation! That

[1] From *Studies in the Scriptures*, part of his last annual letter. The author died on July 15, 1952, but his wife, using her husband's material already prepared, continued the publication of the magazine until December 1953. Vera Pink, who, with her gift as a typist had always shared in the preparation of the magazine, died on July 17, 1962 in Stornoway. Both their names were appended to the annual letters printed in *Studies*.

vanity of which all of us are so full needs to be beaten down. God has done that very thing, as the context of our opening verse plainly demonstrates. He has singled out the most unlikely and unlovely objects to be his saints and servants—'that no flesh should glory in his presence' (verses 26–29)—that there might be no pretence for boasting. He has further willed and worked to that end by causing the whole of our salvation to be in and from Christ, making him to be our 'wisdom, and righteousness, and sanctification, and redemption' (verse 30).

Oh, the horrible workings of pride, which is ever ready to ascribe unto the creature that which is due to the Creator alone. Boasting ill becomes a beggar who is entirely dependent upon the Divine charity. In 2 Corinthians 10:17, our exhortation occurs again, and here it has a particular application to preachers. Paul had occasion to make reference to his own experiences and labours: he not only did so reluctantly and with reserve, but kept before him this injunction, 'He that glorieth, let him glory in the Lord.' This shows that ministers of the gospel need to be especially careful not to glory in their performances, but instead to give thanks to God for their success: all must be credited to his enabling and blessing. They must not glory in their abilities, attainments or achievements, but only in the Author and Giver of the same. Yet how difficult it is for any of them to recount what the Lord has been pleased to work by and through them without the flesh rising up and claiming part of the honours. Everything must be traced back to God's sovereign goodness: to his special favour, his all-sufficient grace, his unceasing faithfulness, his longsuffering toward us. Even when our duty has been performed, we are but 'unprofitable servants' [*Luke* 17:10]!

'He that glorieth, let him glory in the Lord' are the words that ring in our ears, and it is with them before us that we now desire to write. This issue of the *Studies* completes not only another year, but another decade—the third in its history.

Thirty years are quite a slice out of the average span of life, and it is no easy task to continue writing day by day, month by month and year by year for many of the same readers. Very few realize the vast amount of time and labour which is involved in composing a monthly magazine of this size and character. Every article has hours of hard work in it, for we do not just scribble down the first things that enter our mind. Moreover, writing sixty articles each year for several hundreds who have had at least half, and probably fifty who possess the whole, of the previous volumes, and to prepare fresh articles for *them*, would be impossible unless the Word of God were inexhaustible. Yet to do so requires *increasing* thought and study in order to bring out of the Divine treasury things new and old. To maintain the standard we have set before us keeps us busy the year round, night as well as day.

As we review this somewhat lengthy ministry, we cannot but marvel at the sovereign and abounding grace of God which has supported and sustained, which has directed and enabled us to compose no less than *two thousand* different articles of varying lengths, averaging four pages each. But those bare figures can convey only a faint idea of the immense amount of toil involved in their preparation, or the strain on our devoted wife as she has typed out the same amid her domestic duties. Truly we serve a great God, and he is greatly to be praised, for during the whole of these thirty years the editor has not had to spend a single day in bed, nor has his wife either for over twenty years past. We have looked definitely to the Lord for the needed health and strength, and he has never failed us. Though we both had the 'flu early this year, by the Divine mercy we were enabled to fight it on our feet, and perform our daily duties.

It should be quite obvious from what has been said above that we have no time available for visiting friends or receiving callers, nor is it possible for us to send private letters every month or so to our readers. We try to write at least once a year to all, and devote several hours a week endeavouring to aid quite a number of young preachers. But we have only one pair of hands and eyes, and are quite unable to meet the desires of some who appear to imagine that we have as much leisure for correspondence as they have. When any require spiritual counsel, or would like us to elucidate anything not clear in our articles, we welcome the opportunity to write to such—though we have no time to spare for controversy. One reason for our remaining in this 'out-of-the-way' (but delightful) place is that we may prosecute our study and work *in quietness* without interruption. We trust that friends will understand our position and realize that the hour we might spend in entertaining, or in writing them an extra letter, is used in preparing a message for over a thousand readers.

We desire neither to be unsociable nor to live the life of a hermit, but we are 'not our own', and are resolved by grace to devote the whole of our energy in an endeavour to feed Christ's lambs and sheep. We highly value such a privilege and honour, and are jealous of anything which tends to encroach upon the same. We are deeply thankful that the Lord has brought us apart from 'the strife of tongues', and has so graciously provided us with a 'peaceable habitation' [*Is* 32:18]. Not that we urge anyone else to follow our example. Others must take their place on the firing line, and each soul should seek to perform his or her duty in whatever position Providence has assigned them. Ours is to seek to send forth messages which, under God, will strengthen the hands of the same, and to pray for those who are bearing the heat and burden of the day. Let God's people be much in supplication for his servants in these perilous times, for many of them are encountering strong opposition and subtle temptations to compromise, while others are greatly discouraged by the coldness and indifference of their hearers.

During the past ten years spiritual conditions in Christendom have not shown any improvement: rather have they markedly deteriorated. Nevertheless, our circulation, though still a very small one when compared with that of more popular religious magazines, *has increased fifty per cent*! Considering the nature of the articles which appear in these pages, that is surely *the Lord's doing*, and it is marvellous in our eyes. It might well be thought that the Depravity articles—so unpalatable to the flesh—would have retarded the gradual enlargement of our coast during the last few years, but, instead, that enlargement has steadily accelerated during the past twenty-four months of their insertion. Is not this another demonstration that God honours those who honour him by withholding nothing that is profitable [*Acts* 20:20] from their hearers or readers? Let young preachers note this, and take courage.

During the whole of these thirty years we have never been in debt a penny, and have paid every bill within forty-eight hours of its reception. Nor have we ever made any appeal, directly or indirectly, for funds. There was not the slightest need to do so. As Hudson Taylor rightly said, 'God's work, done in God's way, will never lack God's supplies.' We have no denomination or organization behind us, no 'sustentation fund' to draw upon. But what is infinitely better, we have the living God to look to, and he has promised to supply all our need. He does more: once again (despite increased costs of publishing) we have a surplus, which we shall use this year in sending to the Trinitarian Bible Society, the Scripture Gift Mission, for the circulation of God's Word, and to the *Gospel Magazine* (69 Fleet Street, London, E.C.4). Will kind friends note that by the goodness of God our personal needs are fully provided for, so please *refrain* from sending money for our own use.

Once more we would heartily thank our prayer-helpers for

their support, and ask for a continuance of their petitions while it pleases the Lord to keep us in this service. 'Not unto us, O Lord, not unto us, but unto thy name give glory' [*Ps* 115:1]. With Christian love,

Yours by divine mercy,